RAND McNALLY

WORLD
CONTEMPORARY
ATLAS
WITH CD-ROM

RAND McNALLY
WORLD
CONTEMPORARY
ATLAS
WITH CD-ROM

CONTENTS

CONTEMPORARY WORLD ATLAS WITH CD-ROM

Copyright © 1996 by Rand McNally & Company.

Printed in the United States of America.

Library of Congress Catalog Card Number: 96-68365

USING THE ATLAS

MAPS AND ATLASES

Satellite images of the world (figure 1) constantly give us views of the shape and size of the earth. It is hard, therefore, to imagine how difficult it once was to ascertain the look of our planet. Yet from early history we have evidence of humans trying to work out what the world actually looked like.

Twenty-five hundred years ago, on a tiny clay tablet the size of a hand, the Babylonians inscribed the earth as a flat disk (figure 2) with Babylon at the center. The section of the Cantino map of 1502 (figure 3) is an example of a *portolan* chart used by mariners to chart the newly discovered Americas. Handsome and useful maps have been produced by many cultures. The Mexican map drawn in 1583 marks hills with wavy lines and roads with footprints between parallel lines (figure 4). The methods and materials used to create these maps were dependent upon the technology available, and their accuracy suffered considerably. A modern topographic map (figure 5), as well as those in this atlas, shows the detail and accuracy that cartographers are now able to achieve. They benefit from our ever-increasing technology, including satellite imagery and computer assisted cartography.

In 1589 Gerardus Mercator used the word *atlas* to describe a collection of maps. Atlases now bring together not only a variety of maps but an assortment of tables and other reference material as well. They have become a unique and indispensable reference for graphically defining the world and answering the question *where*. Only on a map can the countries, cities, roads, rivers, and lakes covering a vast area be simultaneously viewed in their relative locations. Routes between places can be traced, trips planned, boundaries of neighboring states and countries examined, distances between places measured, the meandering of rivers and streams and the sizes of lakes visualized—and remote places imagined.

FIGURE 1

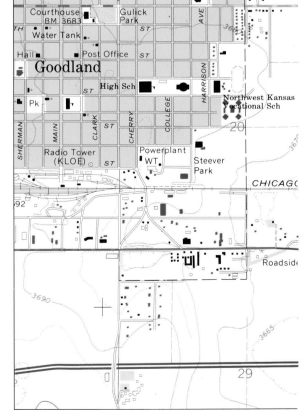

FIGURE 4

FIGURE 2

FIGURE 3

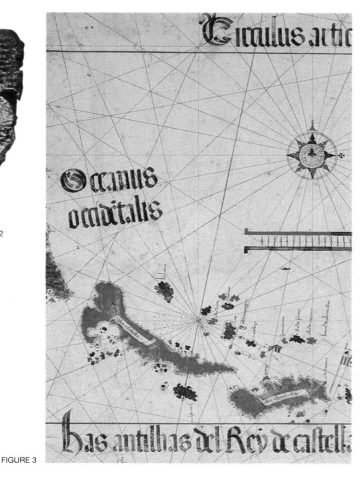

FIGURE 5

SEQUENCE OF THE MAPS

The world is made up of seven major landmasses: the continents of Europe, Asia, Africa, Antarctica, Australia, South America, and North America (figure 6). The maps in this atlas follow this continental sequence. To allow for the inclusion of detail, each continent is broken down into a series of maps, and this grouping is arranged so that as consecutive pages are turned, a continuous successive part of the continent is shown. Larger-scale maps are used for regions of greater detail (having many cities, for example) or for areas of global significance.

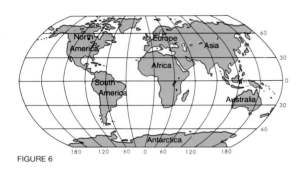

FIGURE 6

GETTING THE INFORMATION

An atlas can be used for many purposes, from planning a trip to finding hot spots in the news and supplementing world knowledge. To realize the potential of an atlas the user must be able to:
1. Find places on the maps
2. Measure distances
3. Determine directions
4. Understand map symbols

FINDING PLACES

One of the most common and important tasks facilitated by an atlas is finding the location of a place in the world. A river's name in a book, a city mentioned in the news, or a vacation spot may prompt your need to know where the place is located. The illustrations and text below explain how to find Yangon (Rangoon), Myanmar.

1. Look up the place-name in the index at the back of the atlas. Yangon, Myanmar can be found on the map on page 38, and it can be located on the map by the letter-number key *B2* (figure 7).

FIGURE 7

2. Turn to the map of Southeastern Asia found on page 38. Note that the letters *A* through *H* and the numbers *1* through *11* appear in the margins of the map.

3. To find Yangon, on the map, place your left index finger on *B* and your right index finger on *2*. Move your left finger across the map and your right finger down the map. Your fingers will meet in the area in which Yangon is located (figure 8).

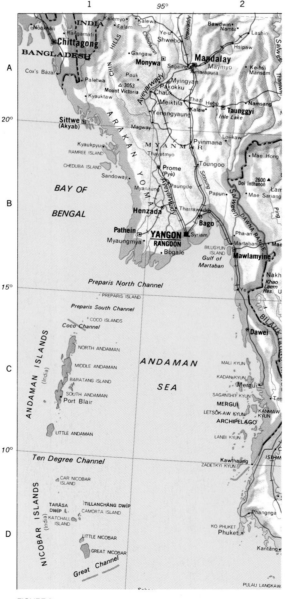

FIGURE 8

MEASURING DISTANCES

In planning trips, determining the distance between two places is essential, and an atlas can help in travel preparation. For instance, to determine the approximate distance between Paris and Rouen, France, follow these three steps:

1. Lay a slip of paper on the map on page 14 so that its edge touches the two cities. Adjust the paper so one corner touches Rouen. Mark the paper directly at the spot where Paris is located (figure 9).

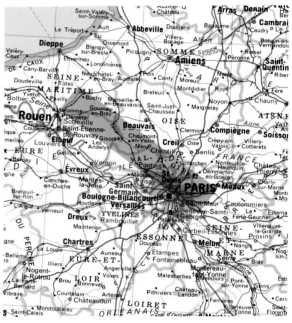

FIGURE 9

2. Place the paper along the scale of miles beneath the map. Position the corner at 0 and line up the edge of the paper along the scale. The pencil mark on the paper indicates Rouen is between 50 and 100 miles from Paris (figure 10).

3. To find the exact distance, move the paper to the left so that the pencil mark is at 100 on the scale. The corner of the paper stands on the fourth 5-mile unit on the scale. This means that the two towns are 50 plus 20, or 70 miles apart (figure 11).

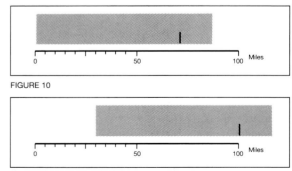

FIGURE 10

FIGURE 11

DETERMINING DIRECTION

Most of the maps in the atlas are drawn so that when oriented for normal reading, north is at the top of the map, south is at the bottom, west is at the left, and east is at the right. Most maps have a series of lines drawn across them—the lines of *latitude* and *longitude*. Lines of latitude, or *parallels* of latitude, are drawn east and west. Lines of longitude, or *meridians* of longitude, are drawn north and south (figure 12).

Parallels and meridians appear as either curved or straight lines. For example, in the section of the map of Europe (figure 13) the parallels of latitude appear as curved lines. The meridians of longitude are straight lines that come together toward the top of the map. Latitude and longitude lines help locate places on maps. Parallels of latitude are numbered in degrees north and south of the *Equator*. Meridians of longitude are numbered in degrees east and west of a line called the *Prime Meridian*, running through Greenwich, England, near London. Any place on earth can be located by the latitude and longitude lines running through it.

To determine directions or locations on the map, you must use the parallels and meridians. For example, suppose you want to know which is farther north, Bergen, Norway, or Stockholm, Sweden. The map in figure 13 shows that Stockholm is south of the 60° parallel of latitude and Bergen is north of it. Bergen is farther north than Stockholm. By looking at the meridians of longitude, you can determine which city is farther east. Bergen is approximately 5° east of the 0° meridian (Prime Meridian), and Stockholm is almost 20° east of it. Stockholm is farther east than Bergen.

UNDERSTANDING MAP SYMBOLS

In a very real sense, the whole map is a symbol, representing the world or a part of it. It is a reduced representation of the earth; each of the world's features—cities, rivers, etc.—is represented on the map by a symbol. Map symbols may take the form of points, such as dots or squares (often used for cities, capital cities, or points of interest), or lines (roads, railroads, rivers). Symbols may also occupy an area, showing extent of coverage (terrain, forests, deserts). They seldom look like the feature they represent and therefore must be identified and interpreted. For instance, the maps in this atlas define political units by a colored line depicting their boundaries. Neither the colors nor the boundary lines are actually found on the surface of the earth, but because countries and states are such important political components of the world, strong symbols are used to represent them. The Map Symbols page in this atlas identifies the symbols used on the maps.

FIGURE 12

FIGURE 13

World Time Zones

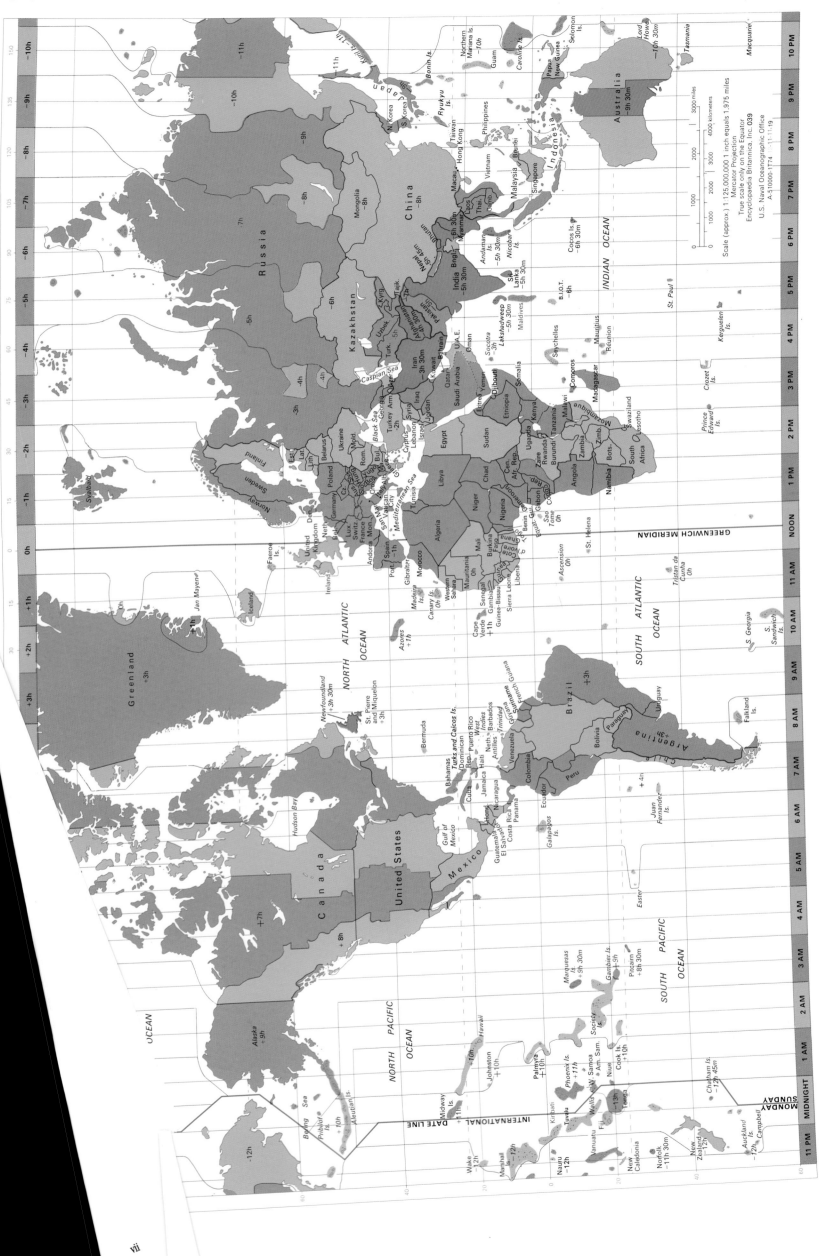

The standard time zone system, fixed by international agreement and by law in each country, is based on a theoretical division of the globe into 24 zones of 15° longitude each. The mid-meridian of each zone fixes the hour for the entire zone. The zero time zone extends 7½° east and 7½° west of the Greenwich meridian, 0° longitude. Since the earth rotates toward the east, time zones to the west of Greenwich are earlier, to the east, later. Plus and minus hours at the top of the map are added to or subtracted from local time to find Greenwich time. Local standard time can be determined for any area in the world by adding one hour for each time zone counted in an easterly direction from

one's own, or by subtracting one hour for each zone counted in a westerly direction. To separate one day from the next, the 180th meridian has been designated as the international date line. On both sides of the line the time of day is the same, but west of the line it is one day later than it is to the east. Countries that adhere to the international zone system adopt the zone applicable to their location. Some countries, however, establish time zones based on political boundaries, or adopt the time zone of a neighboring unit. For all or part of the year some countries also advance their time by one hour, thereby utilizing more daylight hours each day.

Scale (approx.) 1:125,000,000 1 inch equals 1,975 miles
Mercator Projection
True scale only on the Equator
Encyclopaedia Britannica, Inc. 039
U.S. Naval Oceanographic Office
A-510000-1774 - 31-11-19

Time Zones

| h m | hours, minutes |

Standard time zone of even-numbered hours from Greenwich time

Standard time zone of odd-numbered hours from Greenwich time

Time varies from the standard time zone by half an hour

Time varies from the standard time zone by other than half an hour

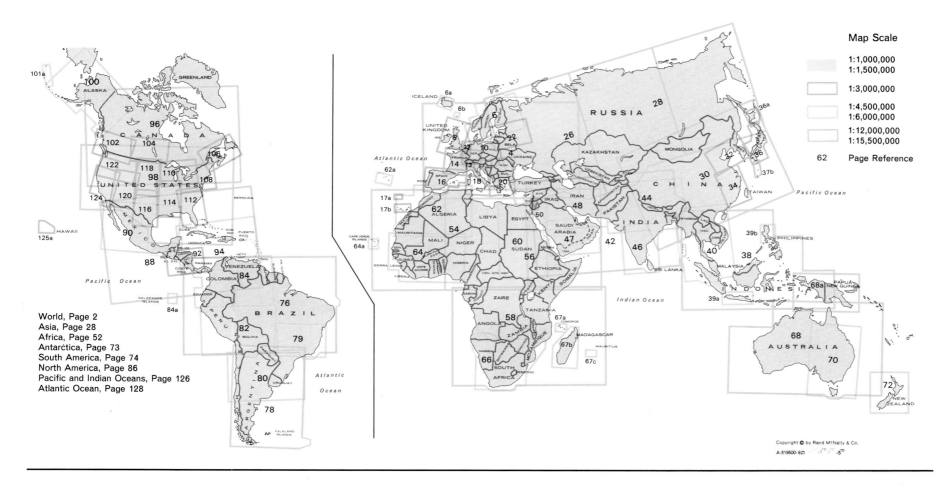

Map Scale

1:1,000,000
1:1,500,000

1:3,000,000

1:4,500,000
1:6,000,000

1:12,000,000
1:15,500,000

62 Page Reference

World Maps Symbols

Inhabited Localities

The size of type indicates the relative economic
and political importance of the locality

Écommoy	Lisieux	**Rouen**
Trouville	**Orléans**	**PARIS**
Bi'r Safâjah °	Oasis	

Alternate Names

MOSKVA
MOSCOW
English or second official language
names are shown in reduced size
lettering

Basel
Bâle

Volgograd
(Stalingrad)
Historical or other alternates in
the local language are shown in
parentheses

Urban Area (Area of continuous industrial,
commercial, and residential development)

Capitals of Political Units

BUDAPEST   Independent Nation

Cayenne   Dependency
(Colony, protectorate, etc.)

Recife   State, Province, County, Oblast, etc.

Political Boundaries

International (First-order political unit)

Demarcated and Undemarcated

Disputed de jure

Indefinite or Undefined

Demarcation Line

Internal

State, Province, etc.
(Second-order political unit)

MURCIA   Historical Region
(No boundaries indicated)

GALAPAGOS
(Ecuador)   Administering Country

Transportation

Primary Road

Secondary Road

Minor Road, Trail

Railway

Canal du Midi   Navigable Canal

Bridge

Tunnel

TO MALMÖ   Ferry

Hydrographic Features

Shoreline

Undefined or Fluctuating Shoreline

Amur   River, Stream

Intermittent Stream

Rapids, Falls

Irrigation or Drainage Canal

Reef

The Everglades   Swamp

RIMO GLACIER   Glacier

L. Victoria   Lake, Reservoir

Tuz Gölü   Salt Lake

Intermittent Lake, Reservoir

Dry Lake Bed

(395)   Lake Surface Elevation

Topographic Features

Matterhorn △
4478   Elevation Above Sea Level

76 ▽   Elevation Below Sea Level

Mount Cook ▲
3764   Highest Elevation in Country

133 ▼   Lowest Elevation in Country

Khyber Pass ⌇
1067   Mountain Pass

Elevations are given in meters.
The highest and lowest elevations in a
continent are underlined

Sand Area

Lava

Salt Flat

| Kilometers | 0 | 1000 | 2000 | 3000 | Km. |
| Statute Miles | 0 | | 1000 | 2000 | 3000 | Mi. |

One centimeter represents 750 kilometers.
One inch represents approximately 1200 miles.
Robinson Projection
Scale 1:75,000,000

Europe

British Isles

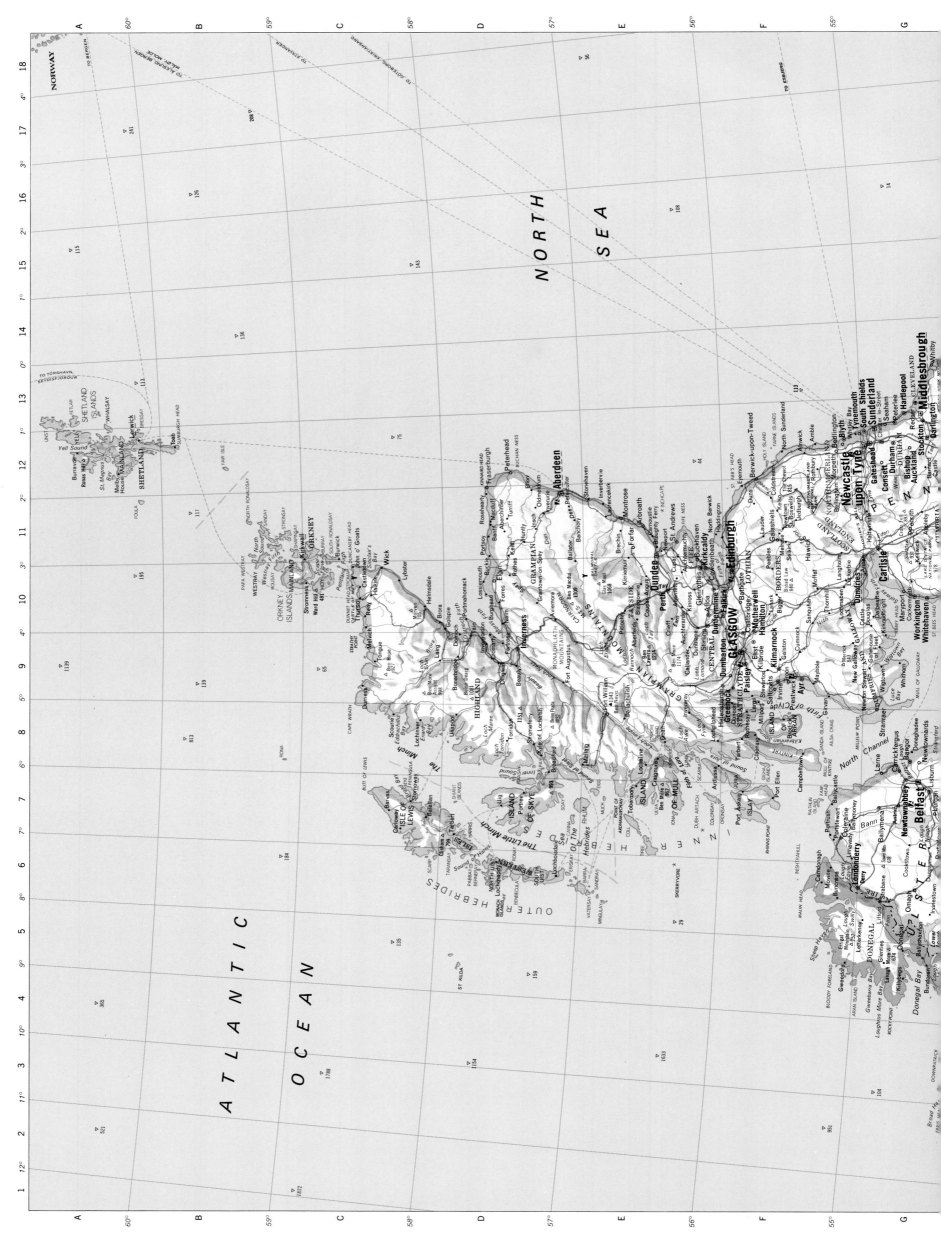

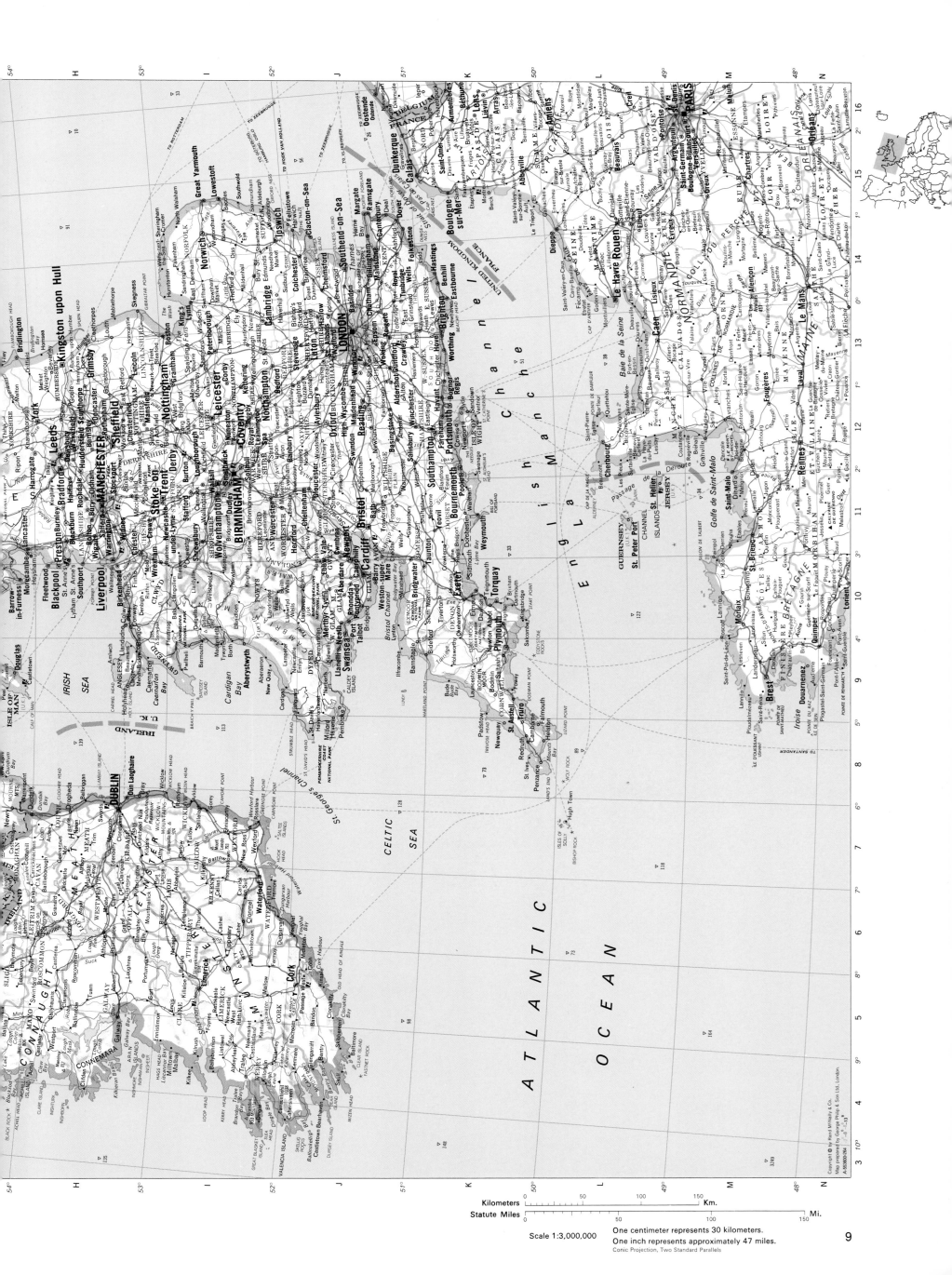

Kilometers

Statute Miles

Km.

Mi.

Scale 1:3,000,000

One centimeter represents 30 kilometers.
One inch represents approximately 47 miles.
Conic Projection, Two Standard Parallels

Kilometers

Statute Miles

Scale 1:3,000,000

One centimeter represents 30 kilometers.
One inch represents approximately 47 miles.
Conic Projection, Two Standard Parallels.

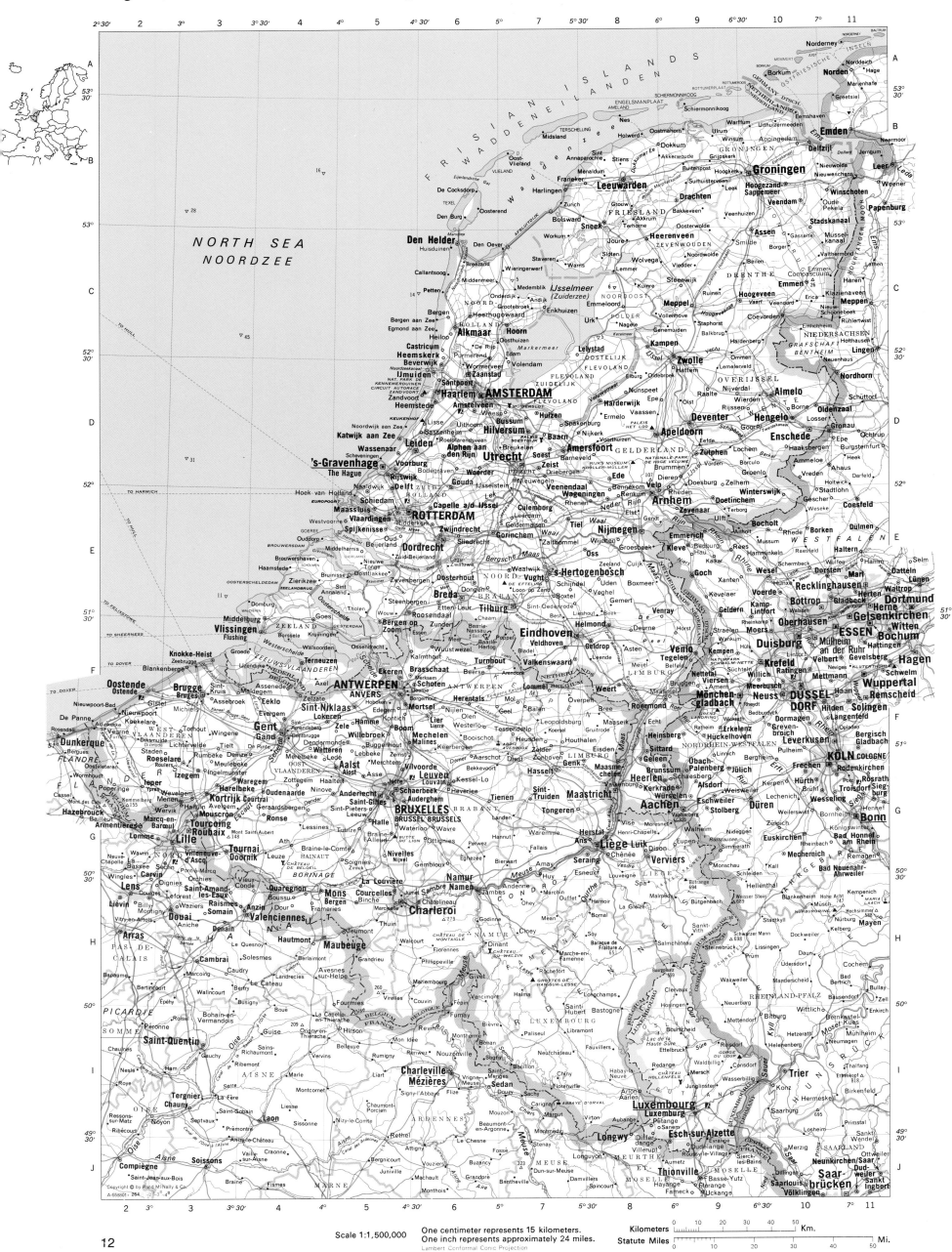

Scale 1:1,500,000

One centimeter represents 15 kilometers.
One inch represents approximately 24 miles.
Lambert Conformal Conic Projection

Kilometers
0   10   20   30   40   50   Km.

Statute Miles
0   10   20   30   40   50   Mi.

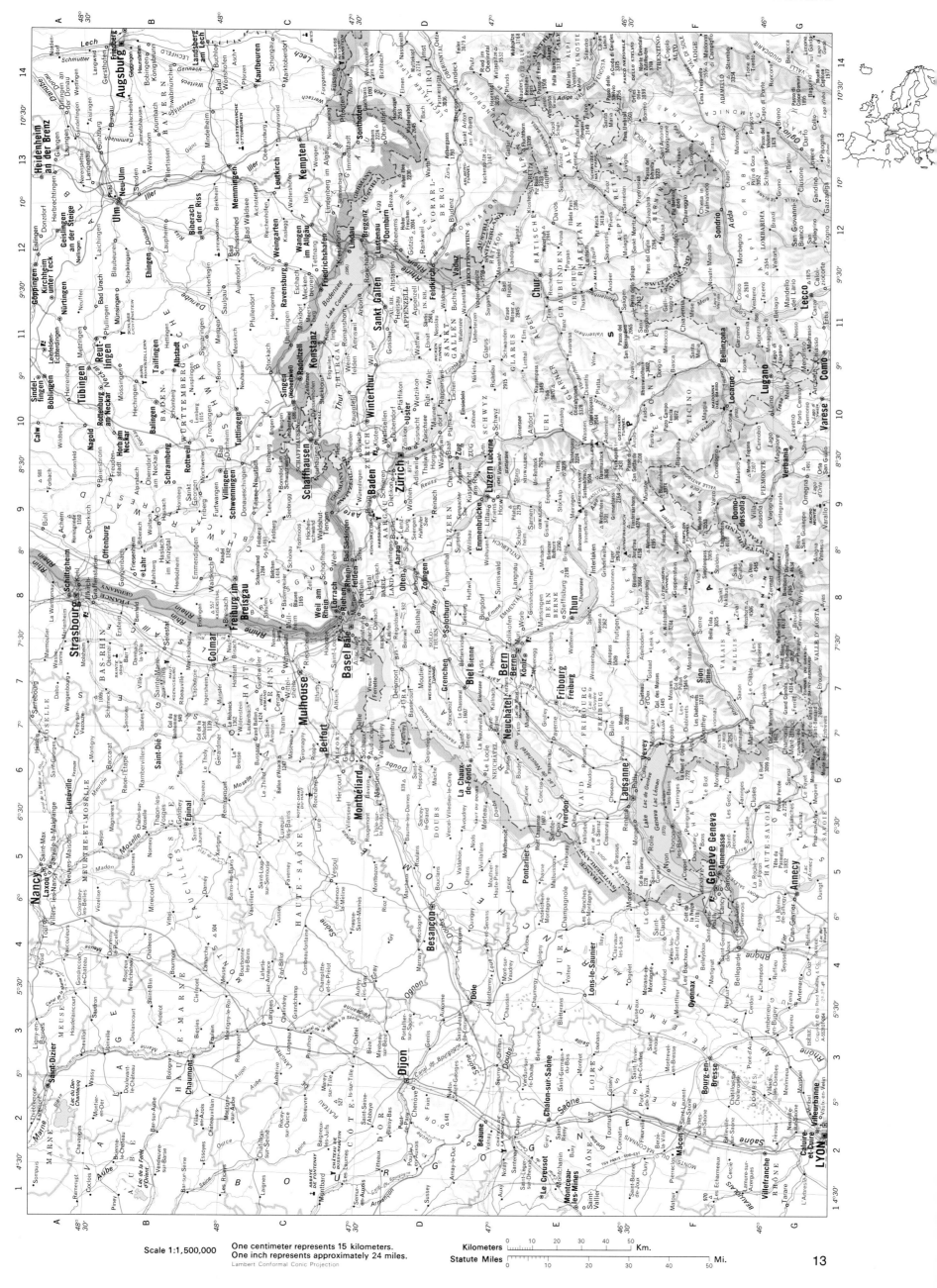

Scale 1:1,500,000
One centimeter represents 15 kilometers.
One inch represents approximately 24 miles.
Lambert Conformal Conic Projection

Kilometers 0 10 20 30 40 50 Km.

Statute Miles 0 10 20 30 40 50 Mi.

Kilometers
Statute Miles

Scale 1:3,000,000

One centimeter represents 30 kilometers.
One inch represents approximately 47 miles.
Lambert Conformal Conic Projection

15

MEDITERRANEAN SEA

Golfe du Lion

ILLES BALEARS
BALEARIC ISLANDS

MENORCA MINORCA

MALLORCA MAJORCA

Palma

EIVISSA IBIZA

FORMENTERA

BALEARS

ATLANTIC OCEAN

ARQUIPÉLAGO DA MADEIRA
MADEIRA ISLANDS
(Portugal)

PORTO SANTO

MADEIRA

Funchal

ILHAS DESERTAS

ISLAS CANARIAS
CANARY ISLANDS
(Spain)

LA PALMA

TENERIFE

Santa Cruz de Tenerife

LA GOMERA

GRAN CANARIA

Las Palmas de Gran Canaria

EL HIERRO

FUERTEVENTURA

LANZAROTE

Arrecife

ATLANTIC OCEAN

ALGERIA ALGÉRIE

Wahran Oran

WESTERN SAHARA

Kilometers
Statute Miles

Scale 1:3,000,000
Conic Projection, Two Standard Parallels

One centimeter represents 30 kilometers.
One inch represents approximately 47 miles.

17

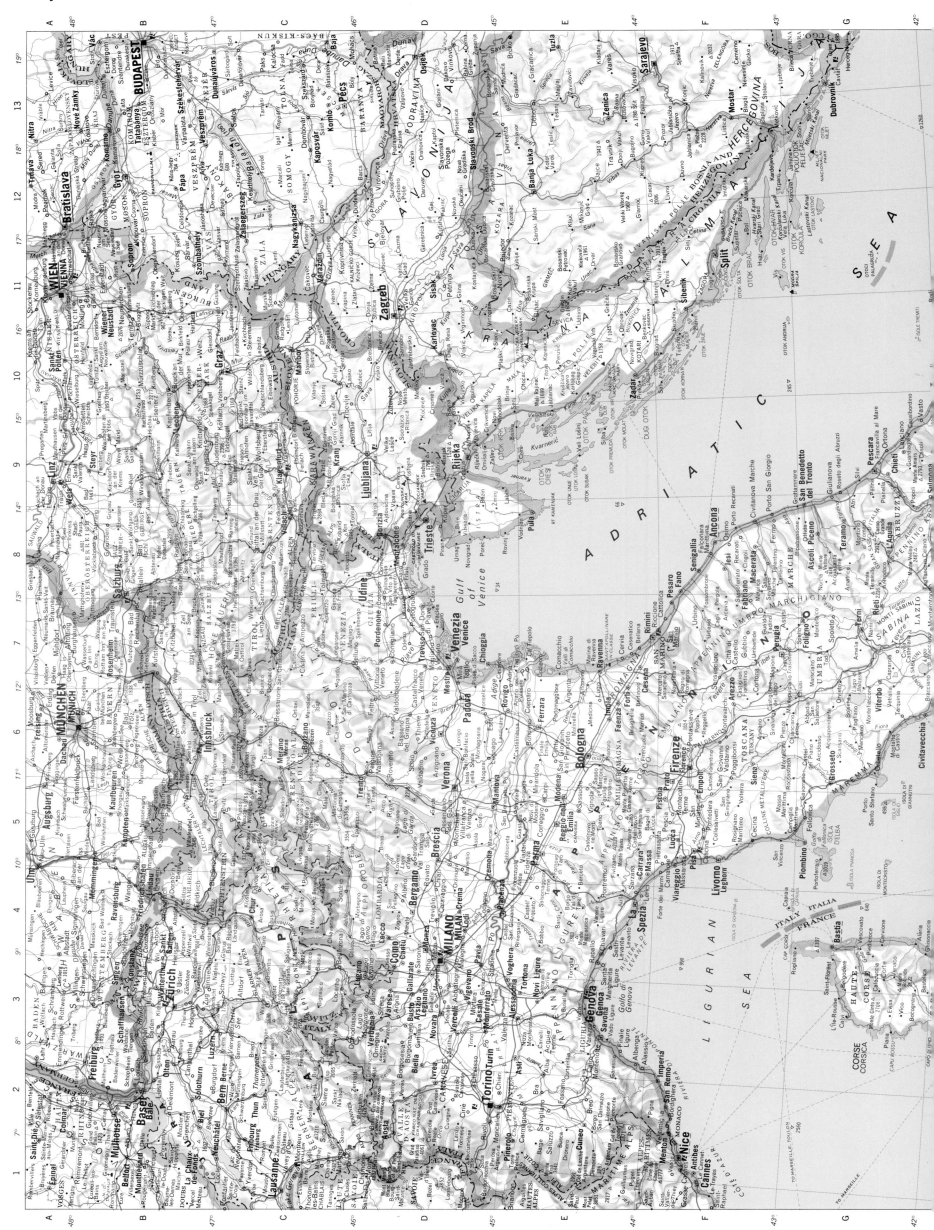

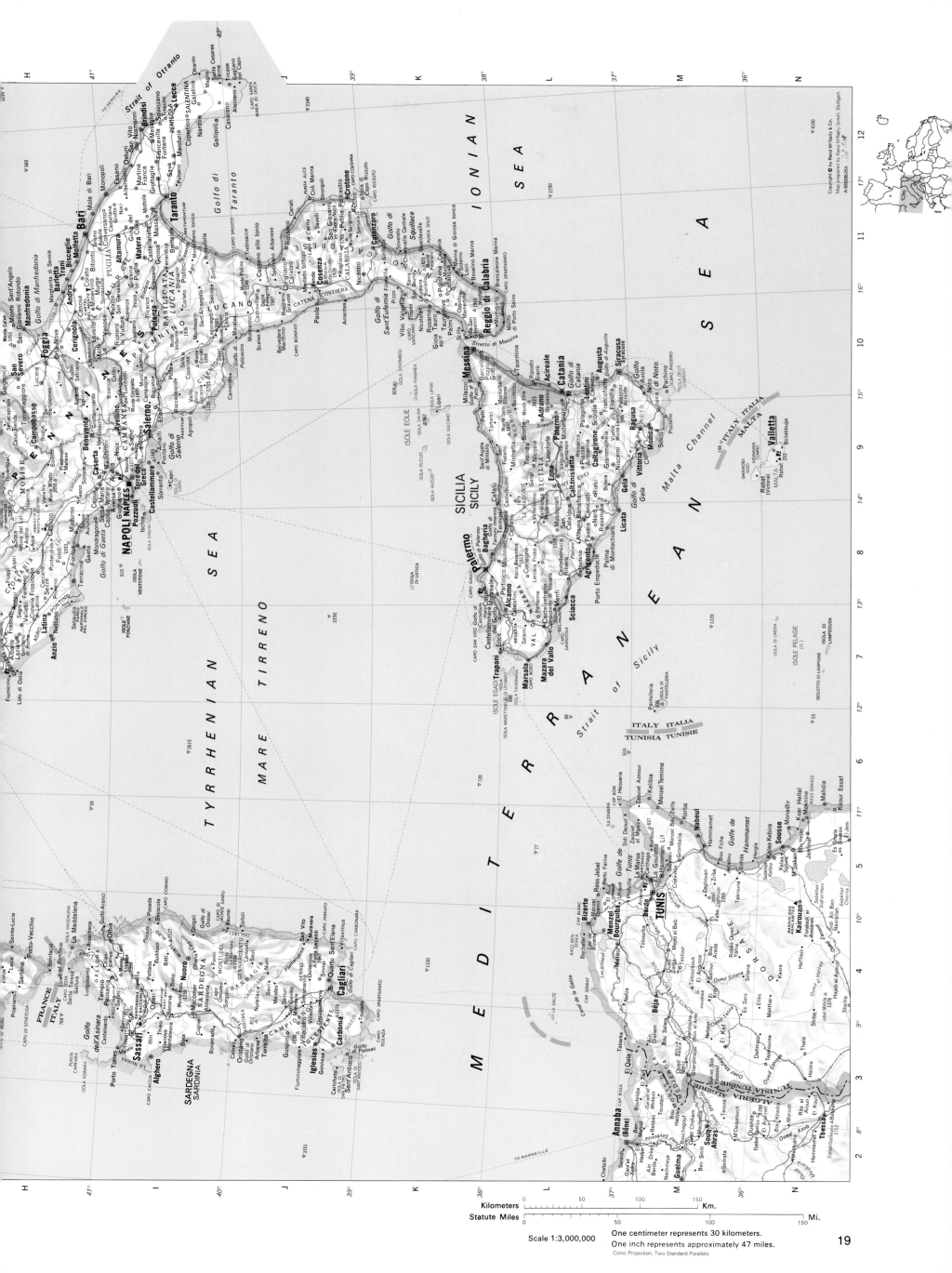

Kilometers

Statute Miles

Scale 1:3,000,000

One centimeter represents 30 kilometers.
One inch represents approximately 47 miles.
Conic Projection, Two Standard Parallels

21

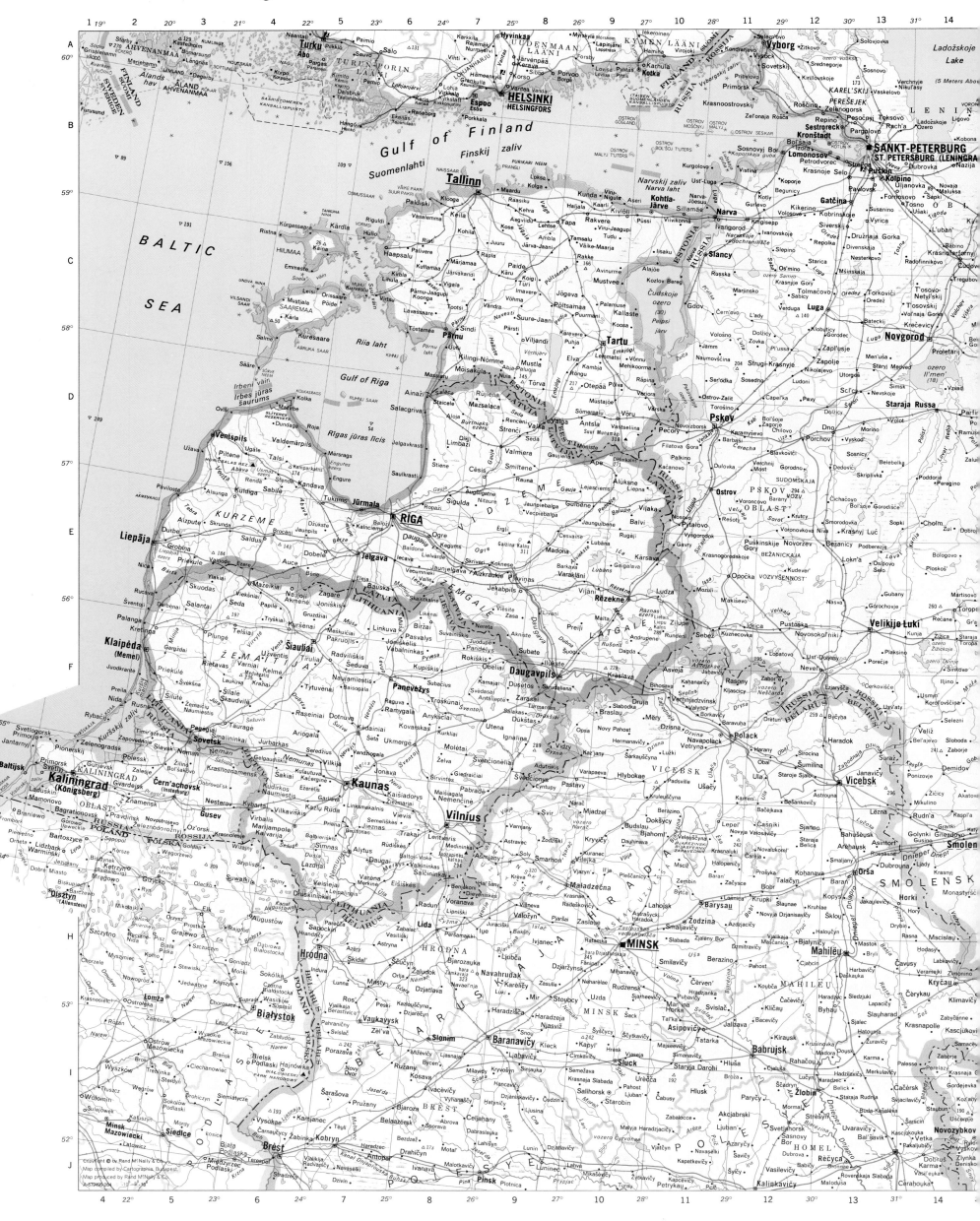

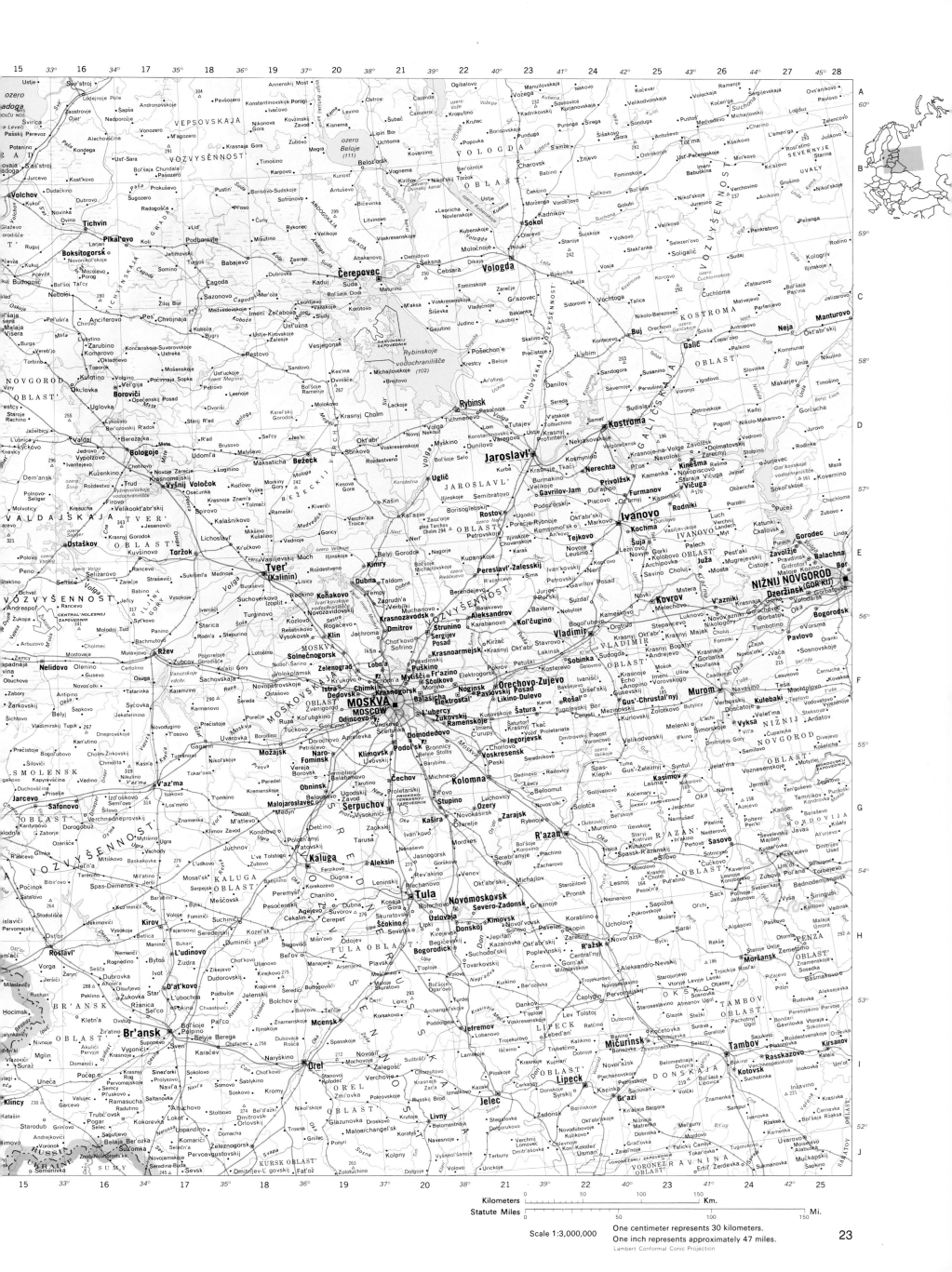

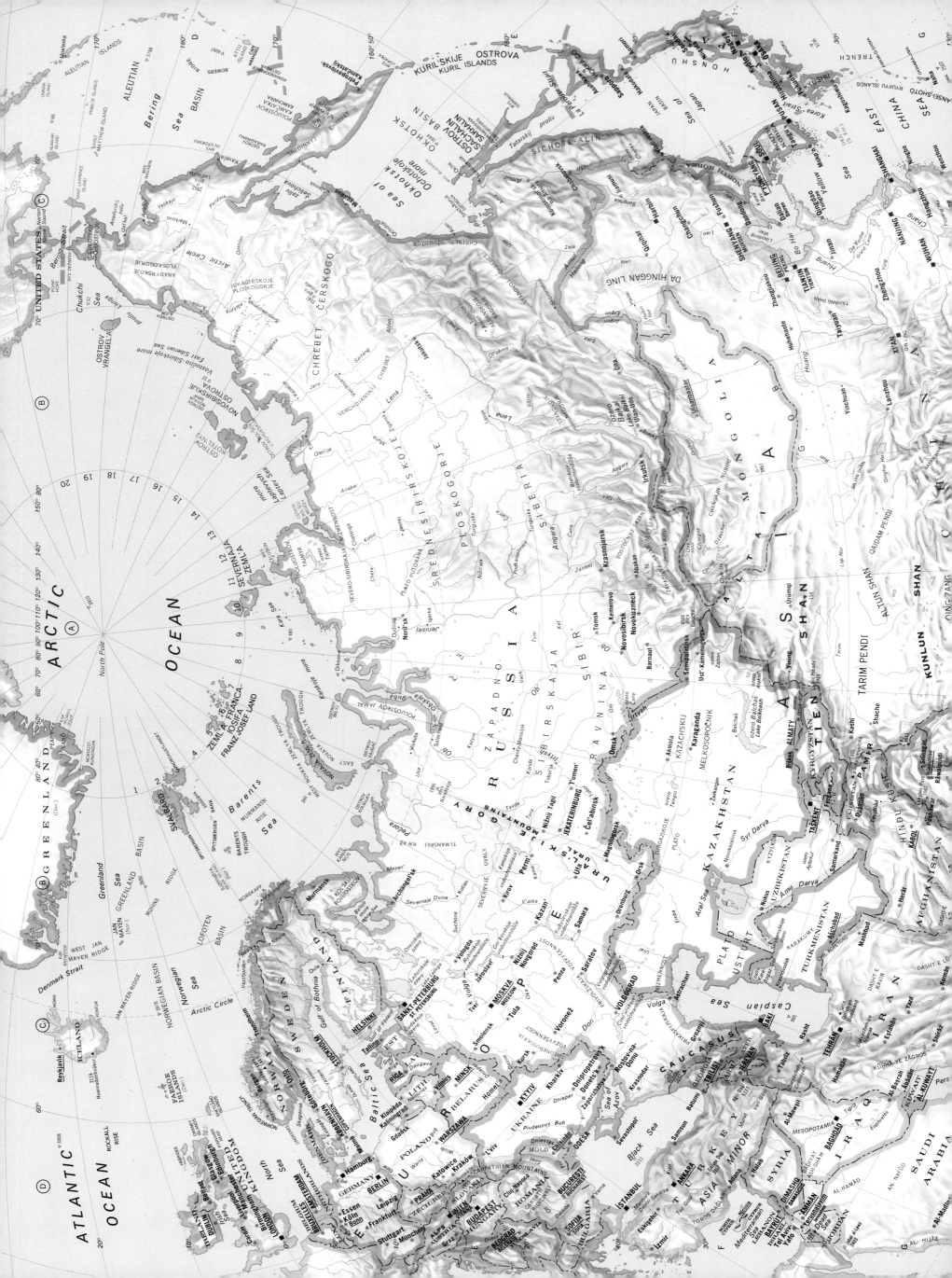

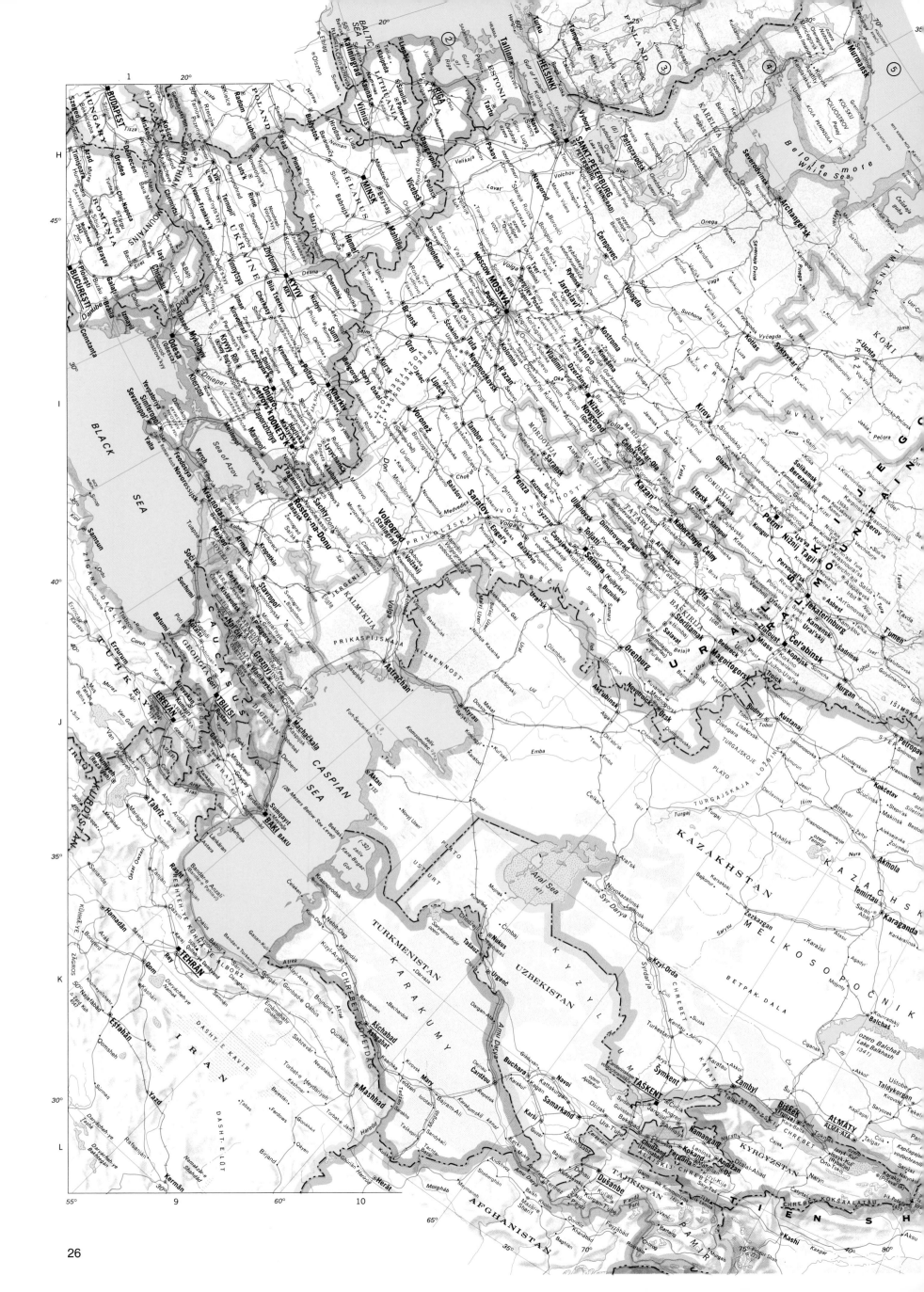

Scale 1:12,000,000

One centimeter represents 120 kilometers.
One inch represents approximately 190 miles.
Lambert Conformal Conic Projection

One centimeter represents 120 kilometers.
One inch represents approximately 190 miles.

Scale 1:12,000,000

Lambert Conformal Conic Projection

Copyright © by Rand McNally & Co.
Map prepared by Esselte Map Service AB, Stockholm
A-579395-264

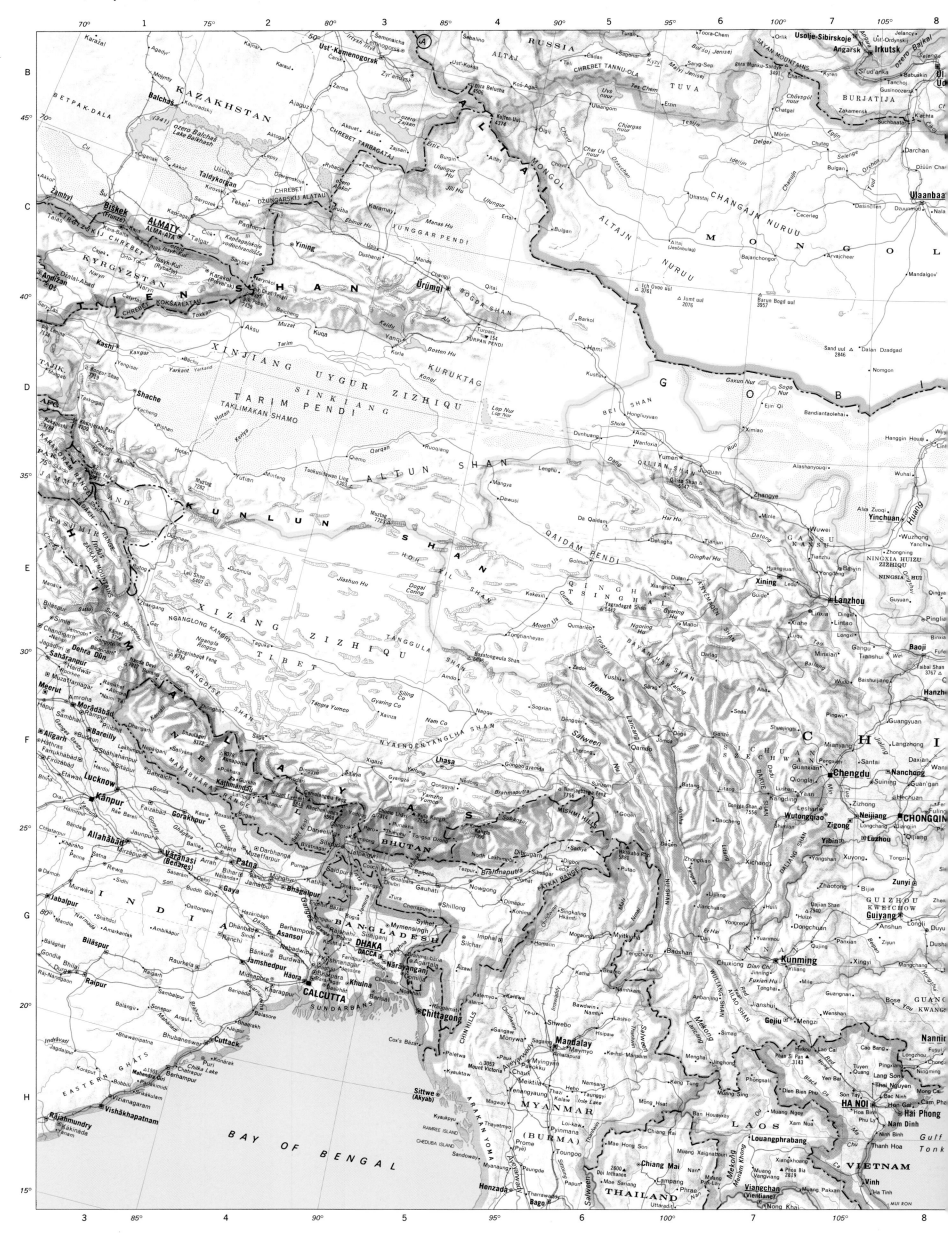

Northeastern China and Korea

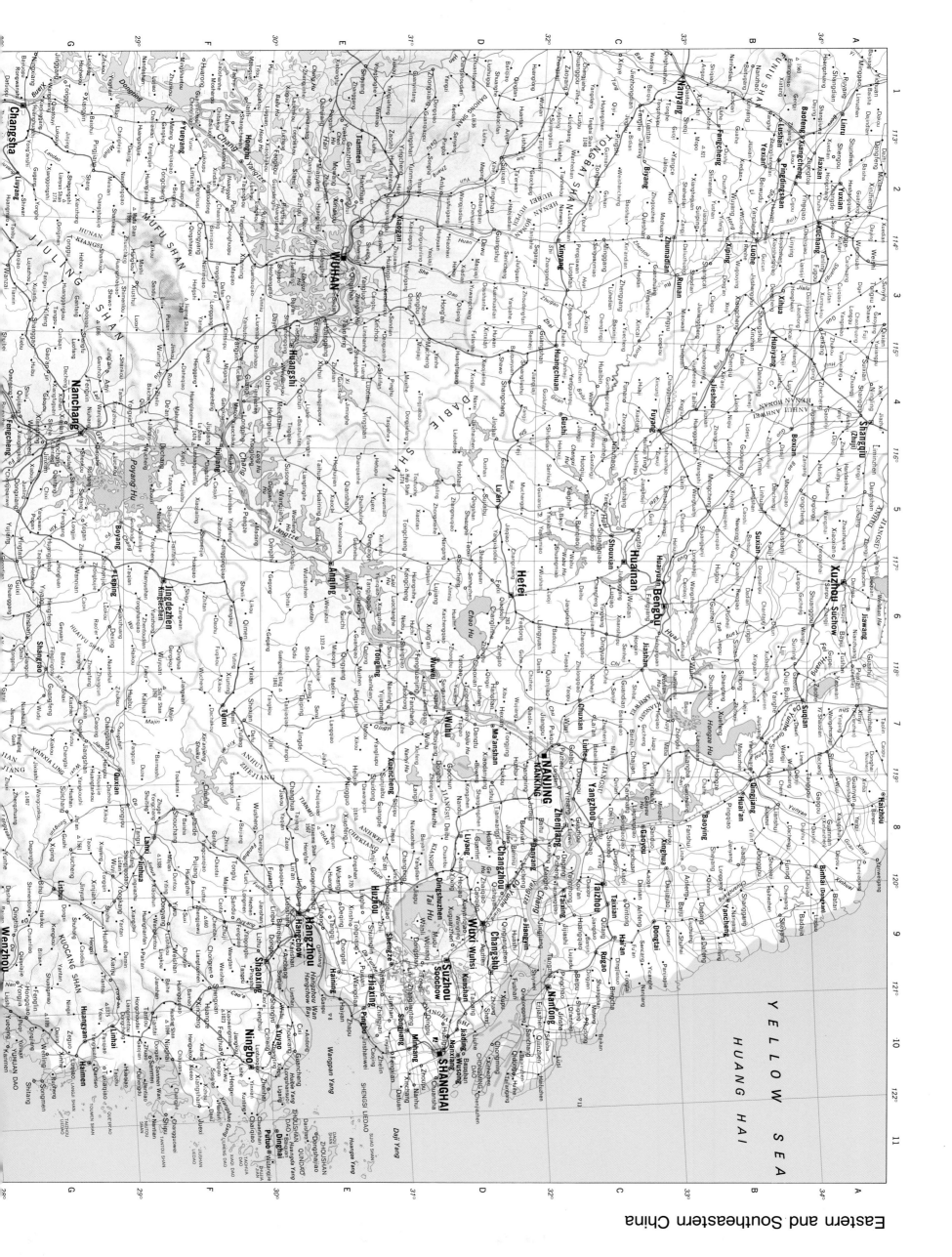

YELLOW SEA

HUANG HAI

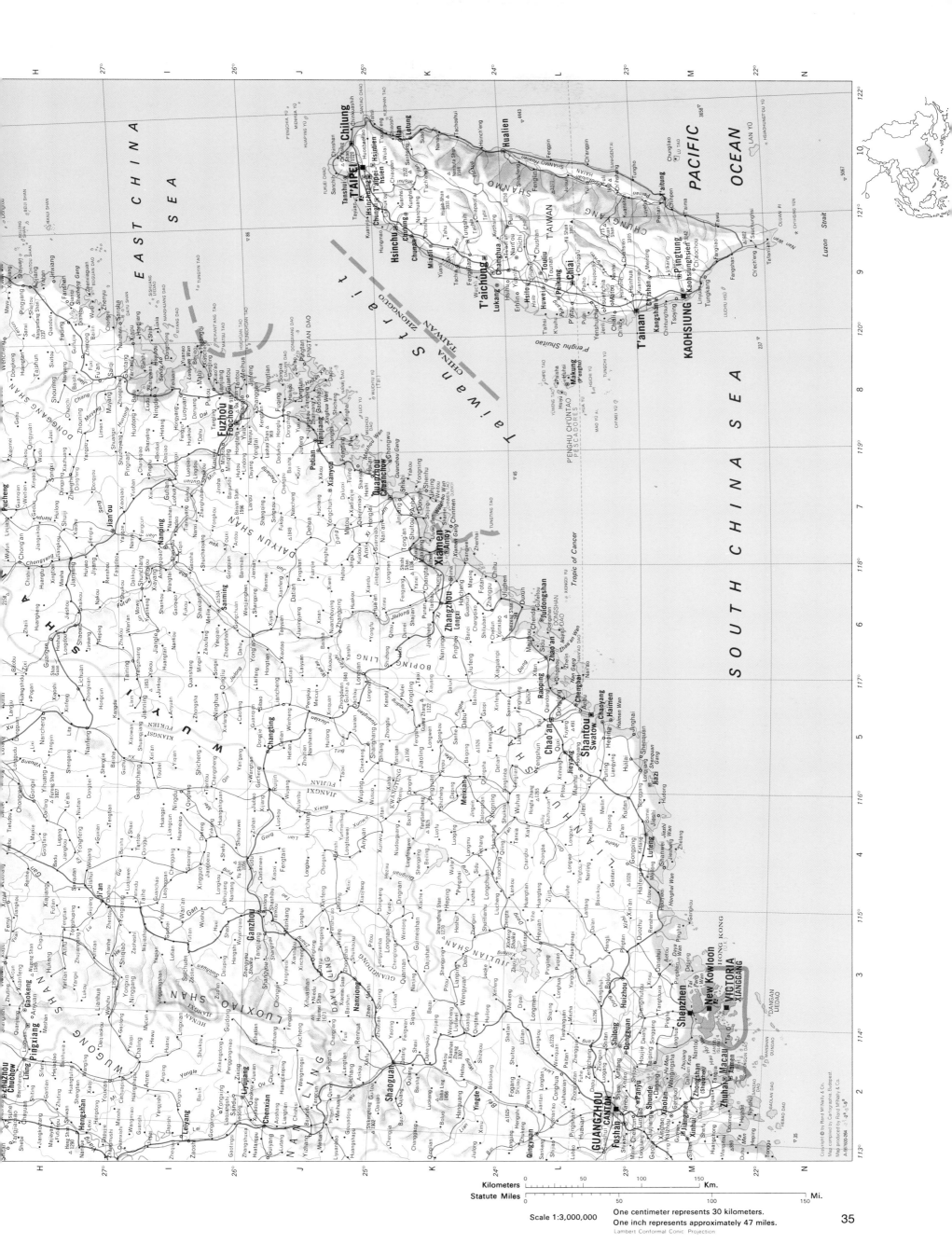

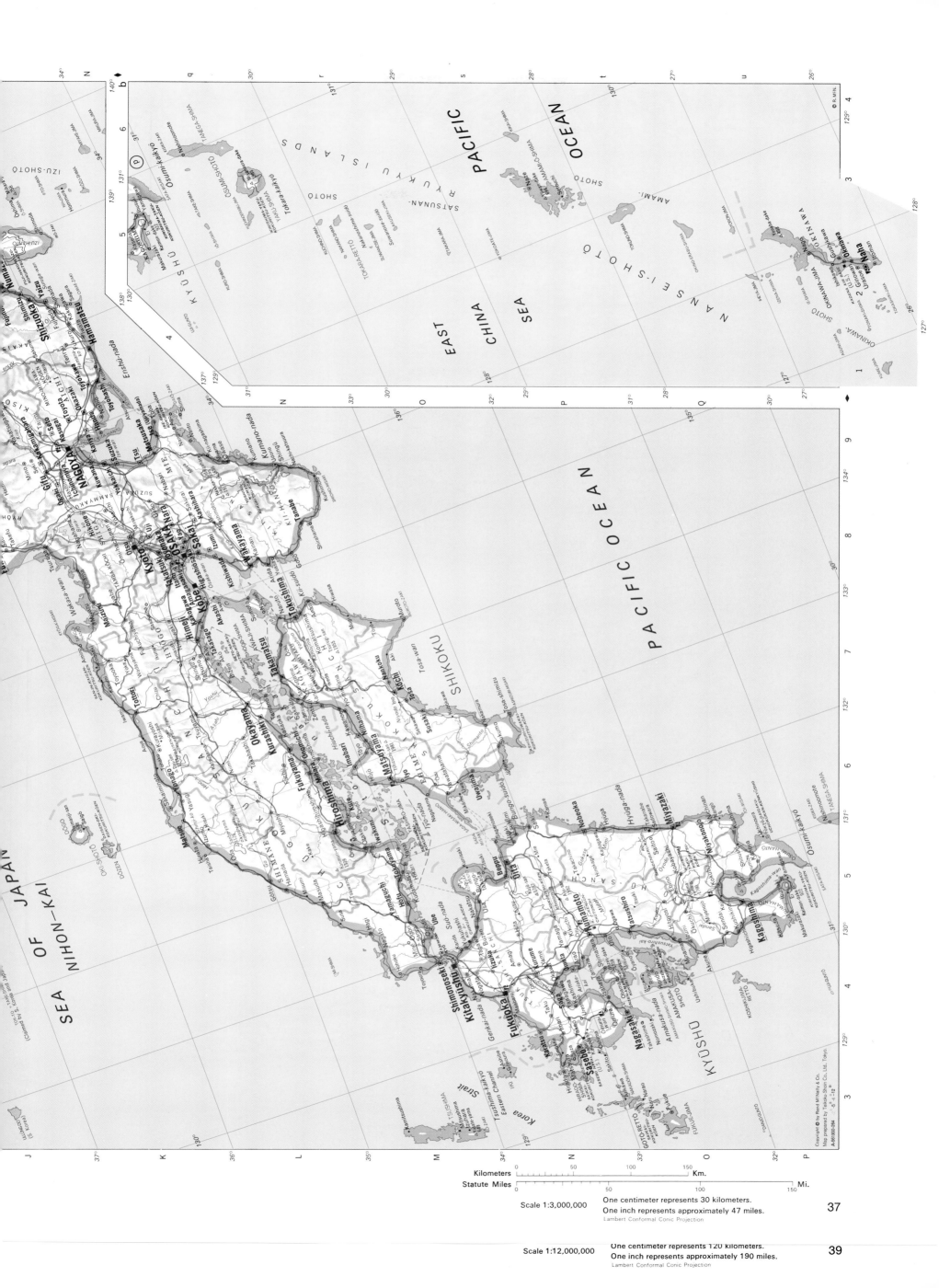

Scale 1:3,000,000
One centimeter represents 30 kilometers.
One inch represents approximately 47 miles.
Lambert Conformal Conic Projection

37

Scale 1:12,000,000
One centimeter represents 120 kilometers.
One inch represents approximately 190 miles.
Lambert Conformal Conic Projection

39

Myanmar, Thailand, and Indochina

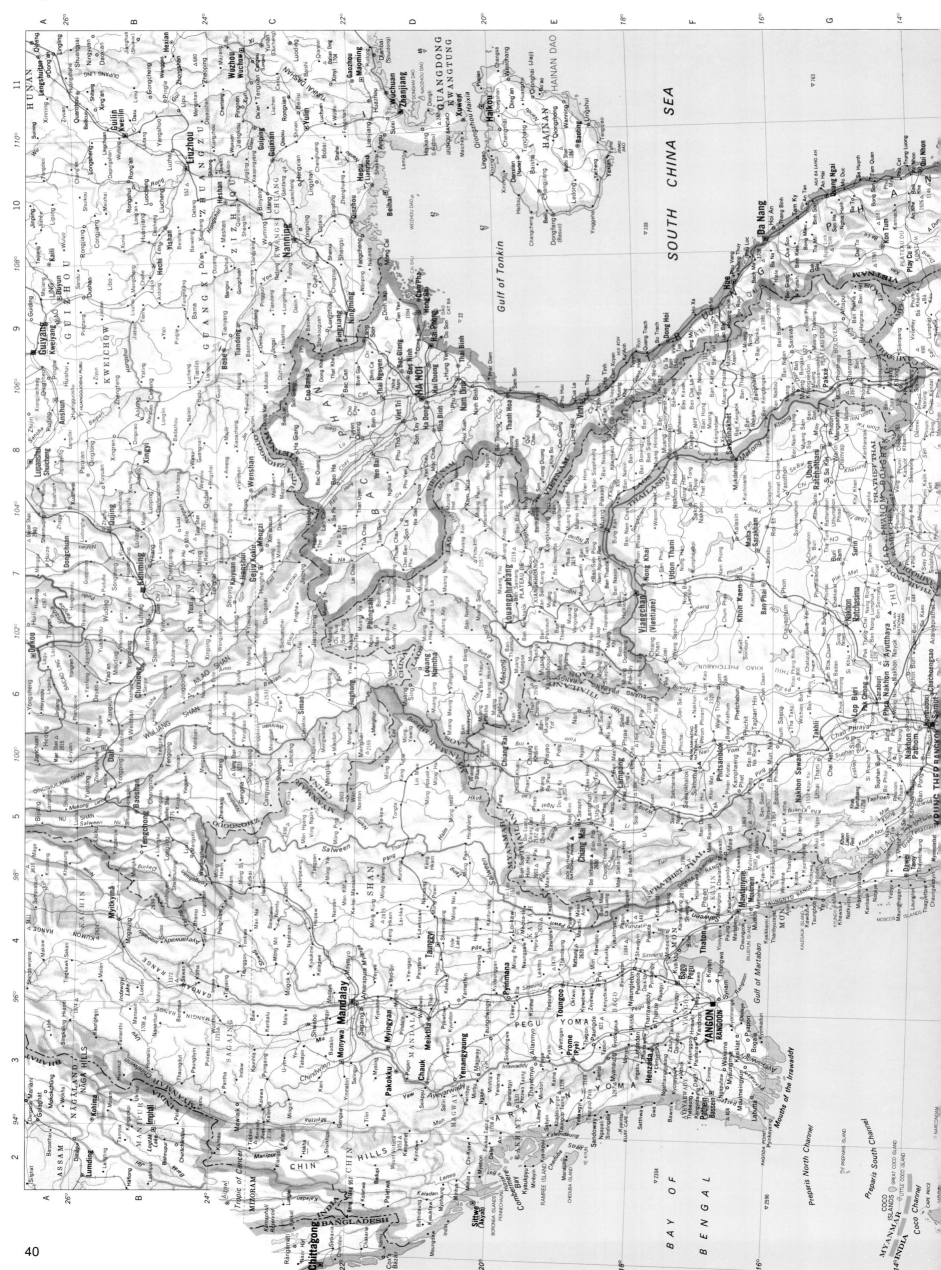

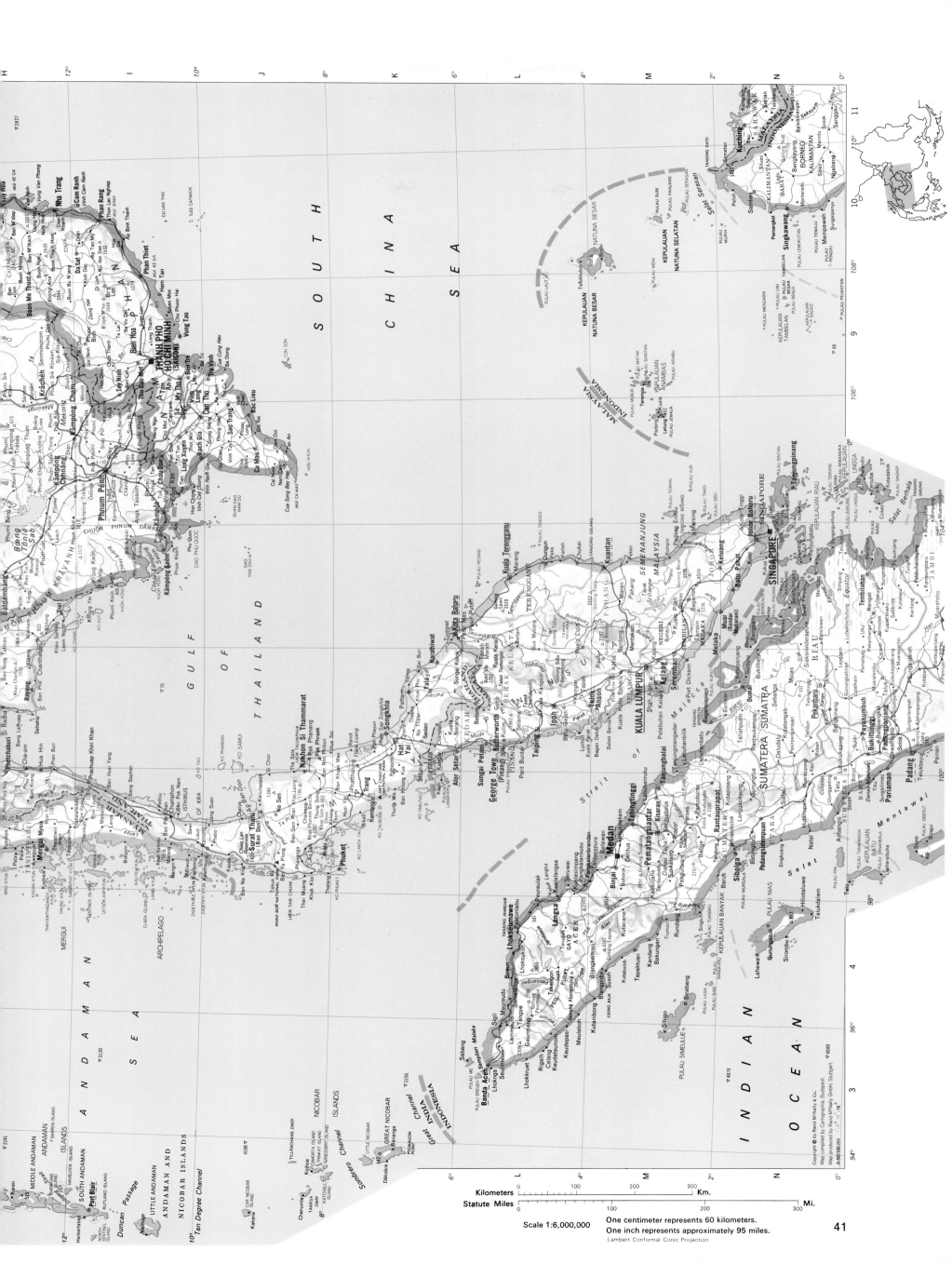

Kilometers

Statute Miles

Scale 1:12,000,000

One centimeter represents 120 kilometers.
One inch represents approximately 190 miles.
Lambert Conformal Conic Projection

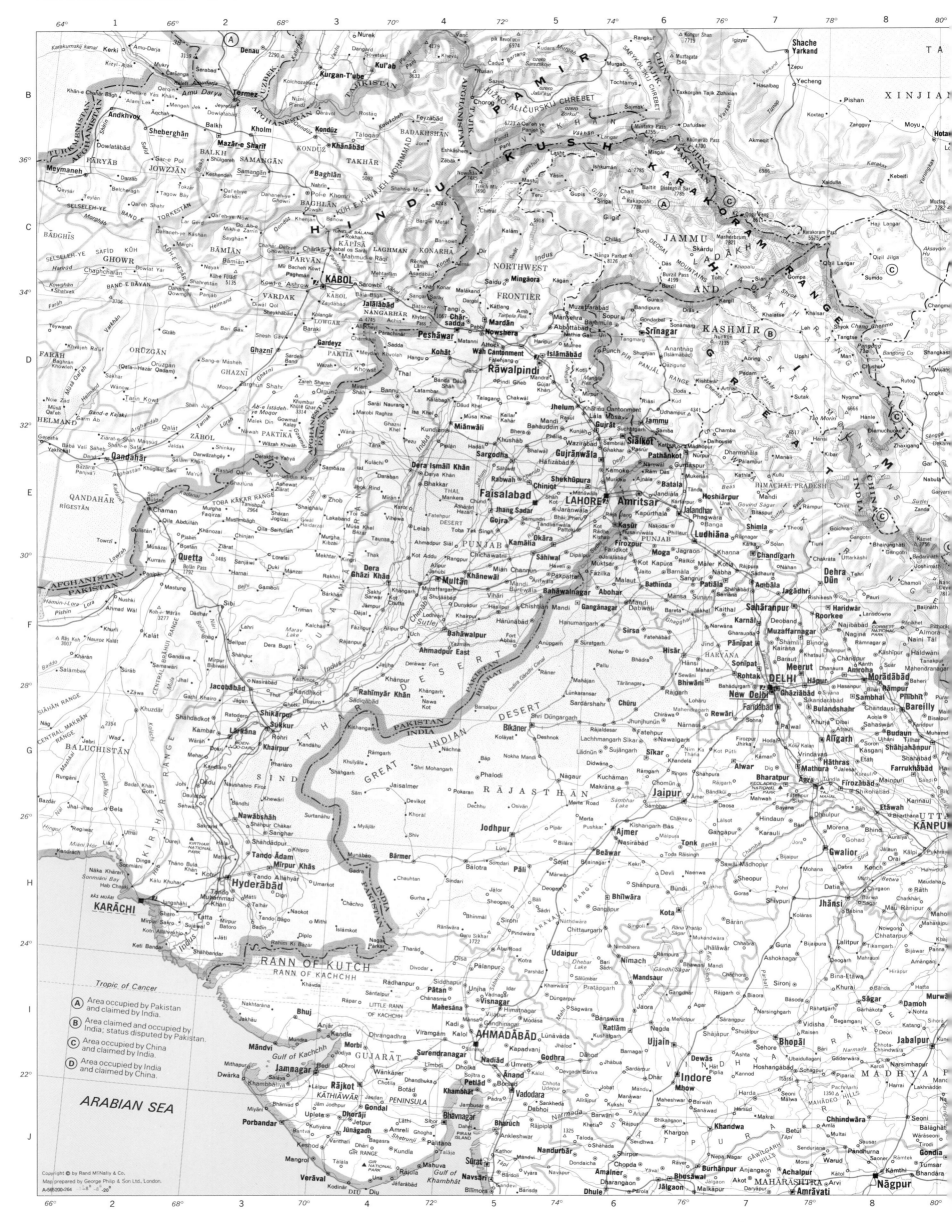

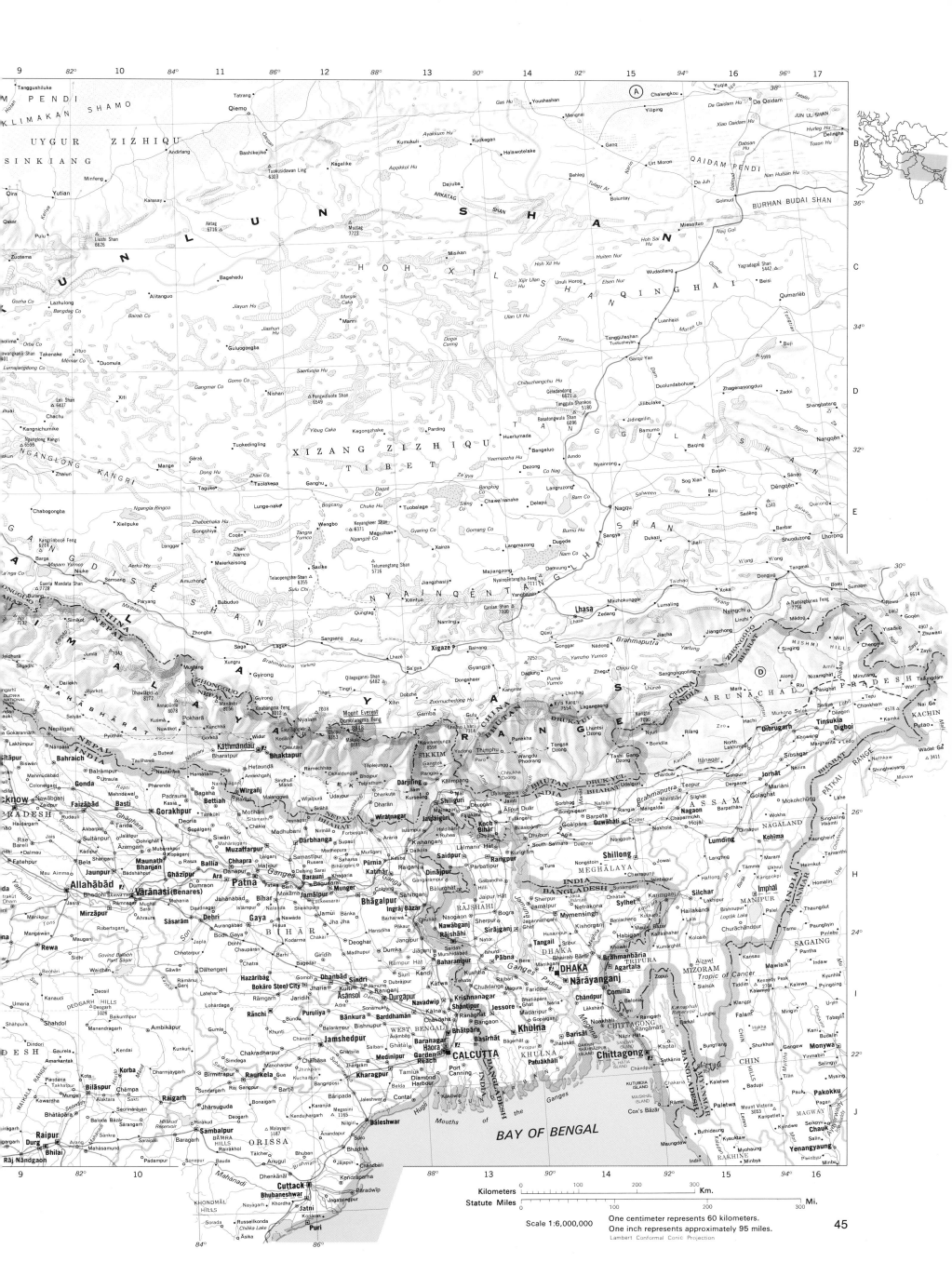

Kilometers
0   100   200   300
Km.

Statute Miles
0   100   200   300
Mi.

Scale 1:6,000,000

One centimeter represents 60 kilometers.
One inch represents approximately 95 miles.
Lambert Conformal Conic Projection

Copyright © by Rand McNally & Co.
Map prepared by George Philip & Son Ltd. London
A-565300-264

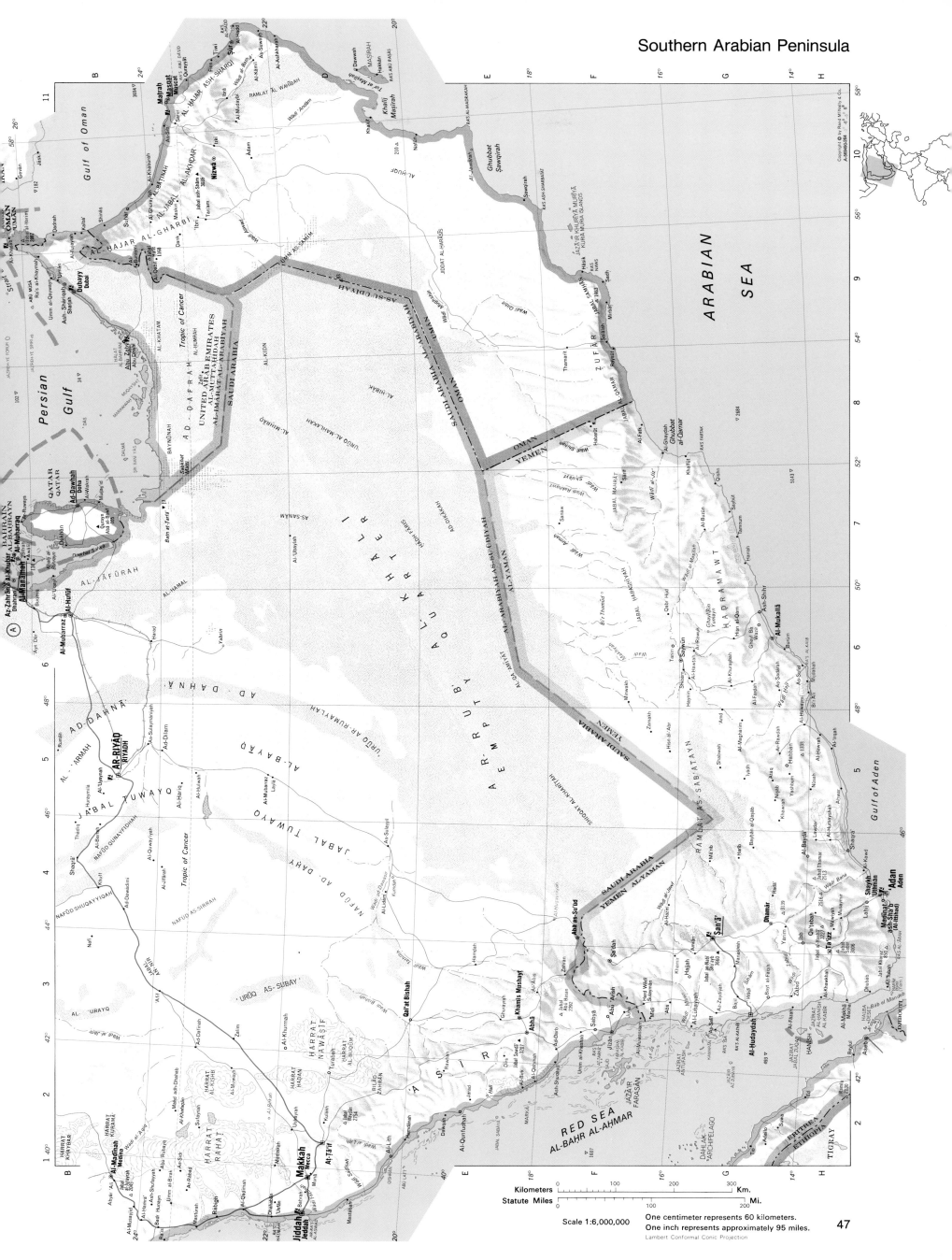

ARABIAN SEA

OMAN

YEMEN

SAUDI ARABIA

AL-'ARABĪYAH AS-SU'ŪDĪYAH

AR-RUB' AL-KHĀLĪ

AD-DAHNĀ'

AR-RIYĀD
RIYADH

Persian Gulf

Gulf of Oman

QATAR

BAHRAIN

UNITED ARAB EMIRATES
AL-IMĀRĀT AL-'ARABĪYAH
AL-MUTTAHIDAH

Tropic of Cancer

Gulf of Aden

RED SEA
AL-BAHR AL-AHMAR

YEMEN
AL-YAMAN

ETHIOPIA

ERITREA

TIGRAY

'Adan
Aden

Makkah
Mecca

Al-Madīnah
Medina

Jiddah
Jeddah

Al-Ţā'if

ḤAḌRAMAWT

Ţ̣UFĀR

Masqaţ
Muscat

Maţraḥ

AL-JABAL AL-AKHDAR

AL-HAJAR AL-GHARBI

AL-HAJAR ASH-SHARQI

Şāna'
Şanā'

Ta'izz

Dhamār

Abhā

Khamīs Mushayţ

Al-Hudaydah

Nizwā

Dubayy
Dubai

Ad-Dawḥah
Doha

Al-Manāmah

Al-Khubar

Az-Zahrān
Dhahran

'ASĪR

Scale 1:6,000,000

Kilometers 0   100   200   300   Km.

Statute Miles 0   100   200   Mi.

One centimeter represents 60 kilometers.
One inch represents approximately 95 miles.

47

Lambert Conformal Conic Projection

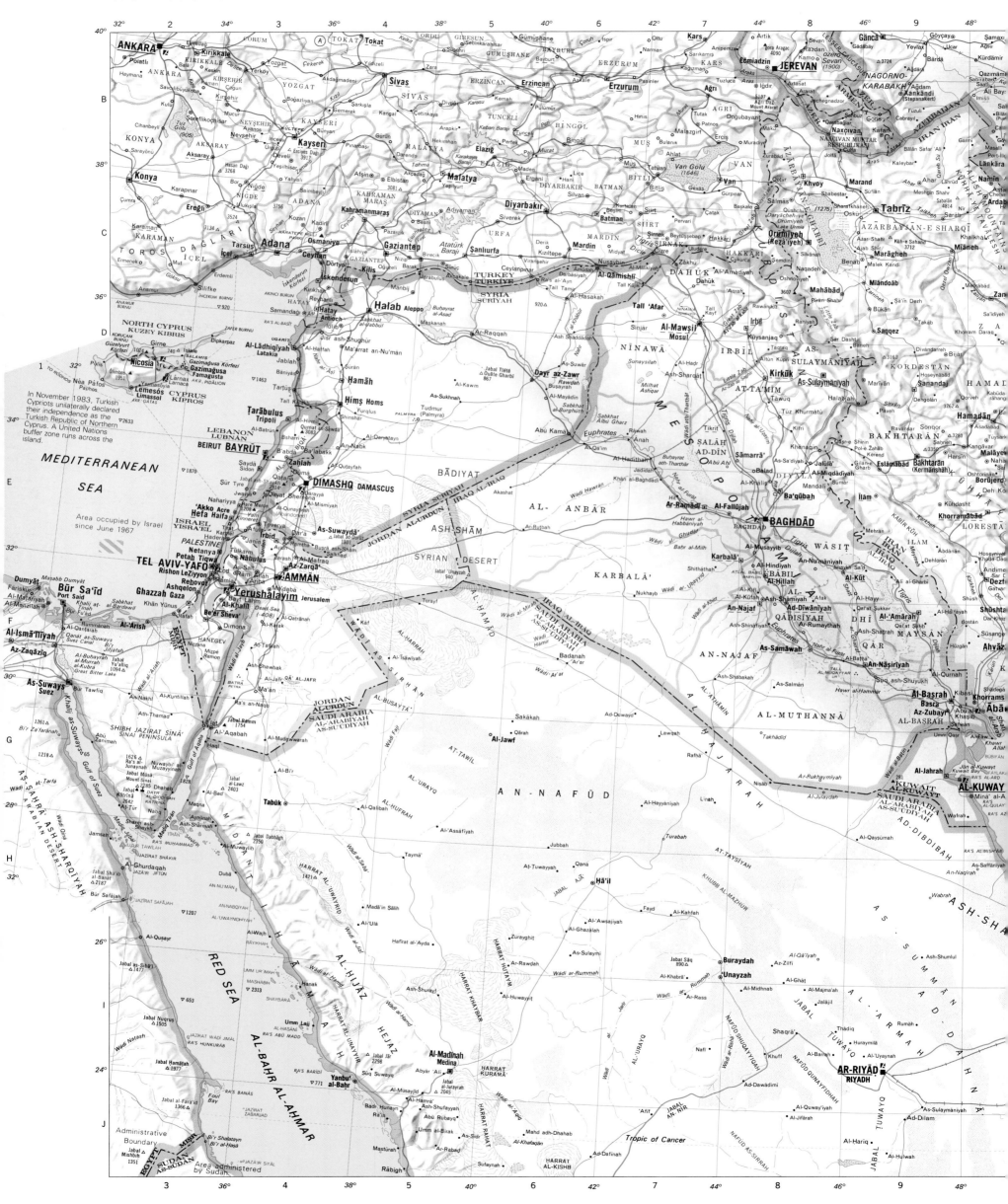

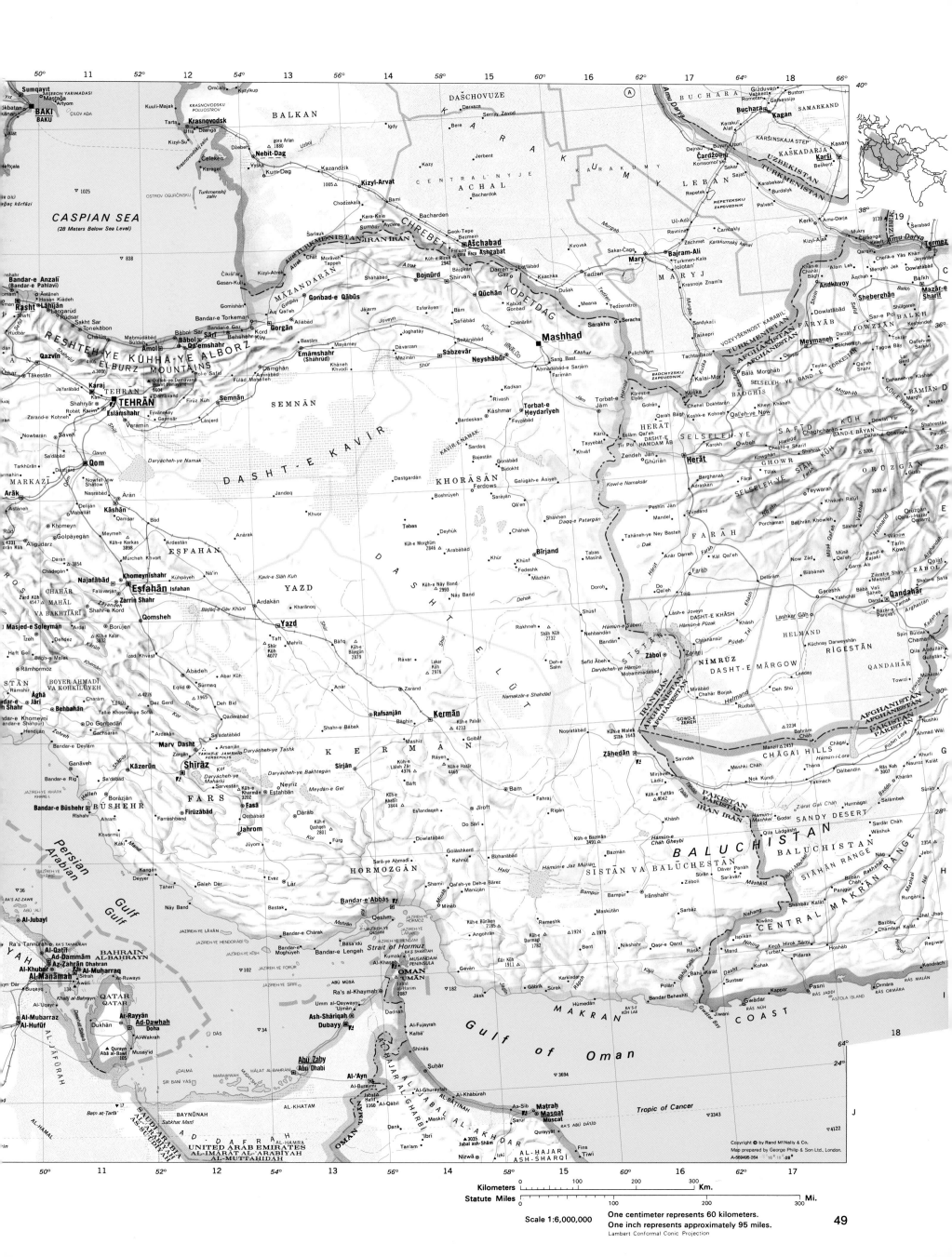

49

Israel and Southern Lebanon

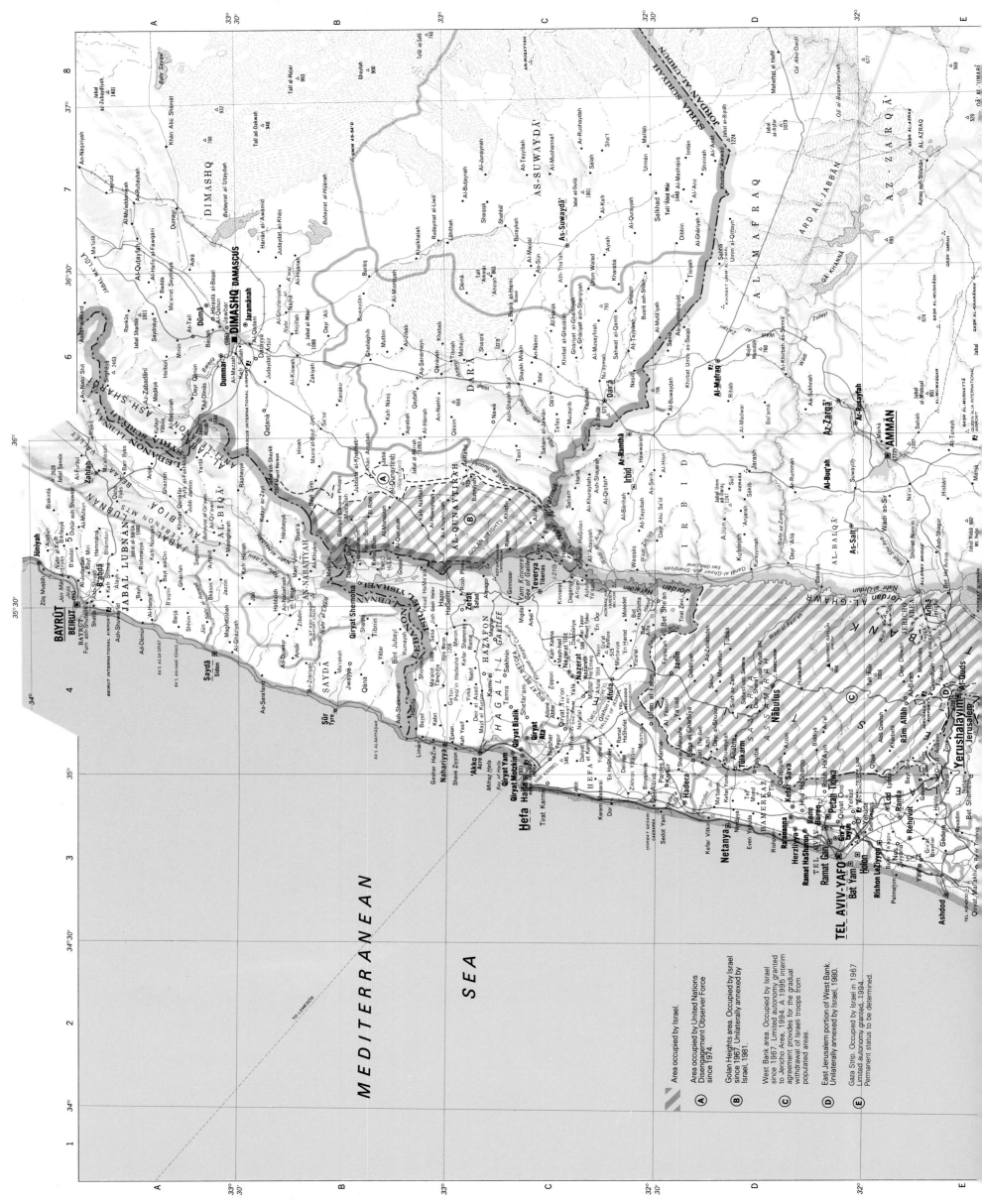

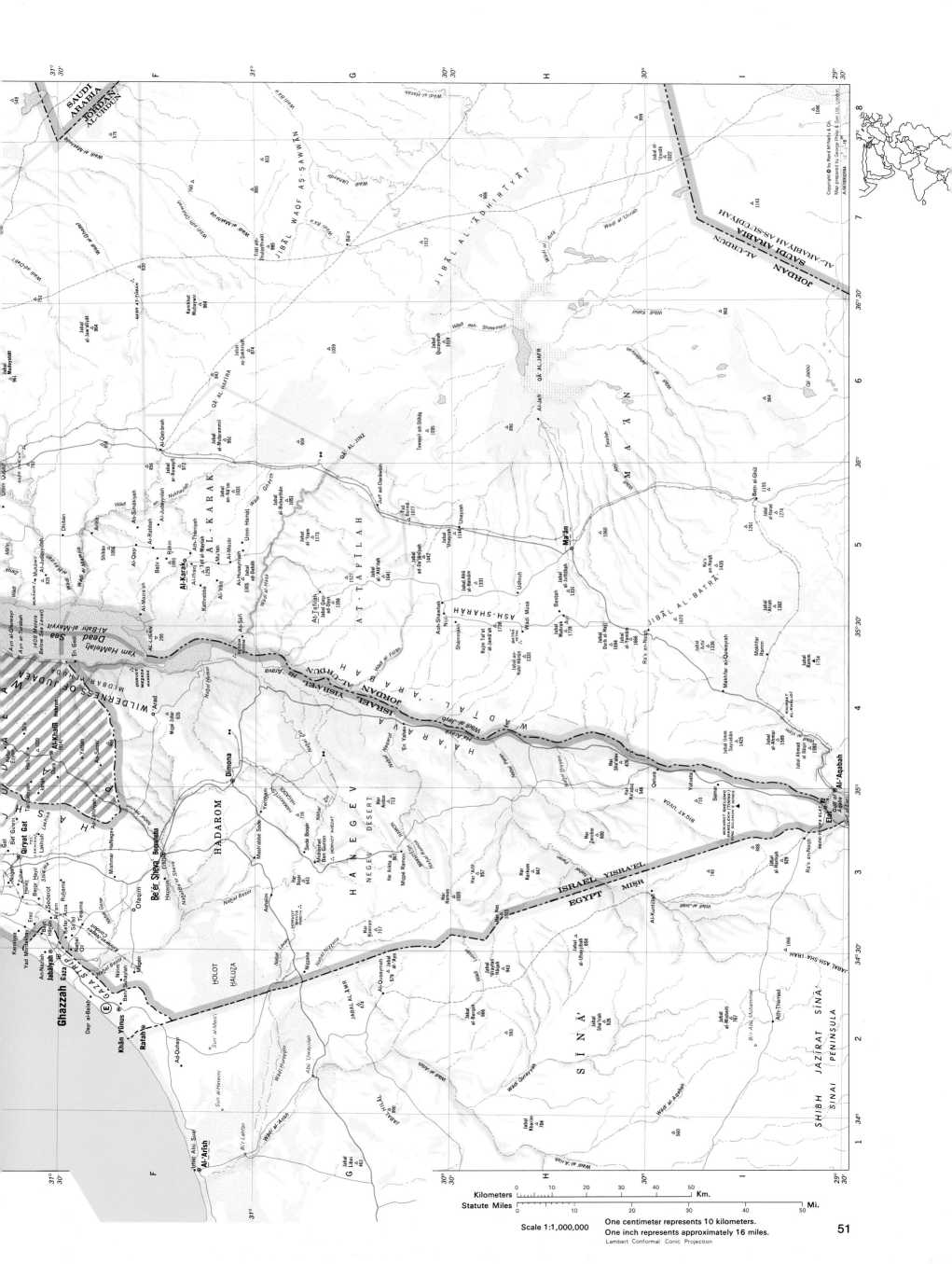

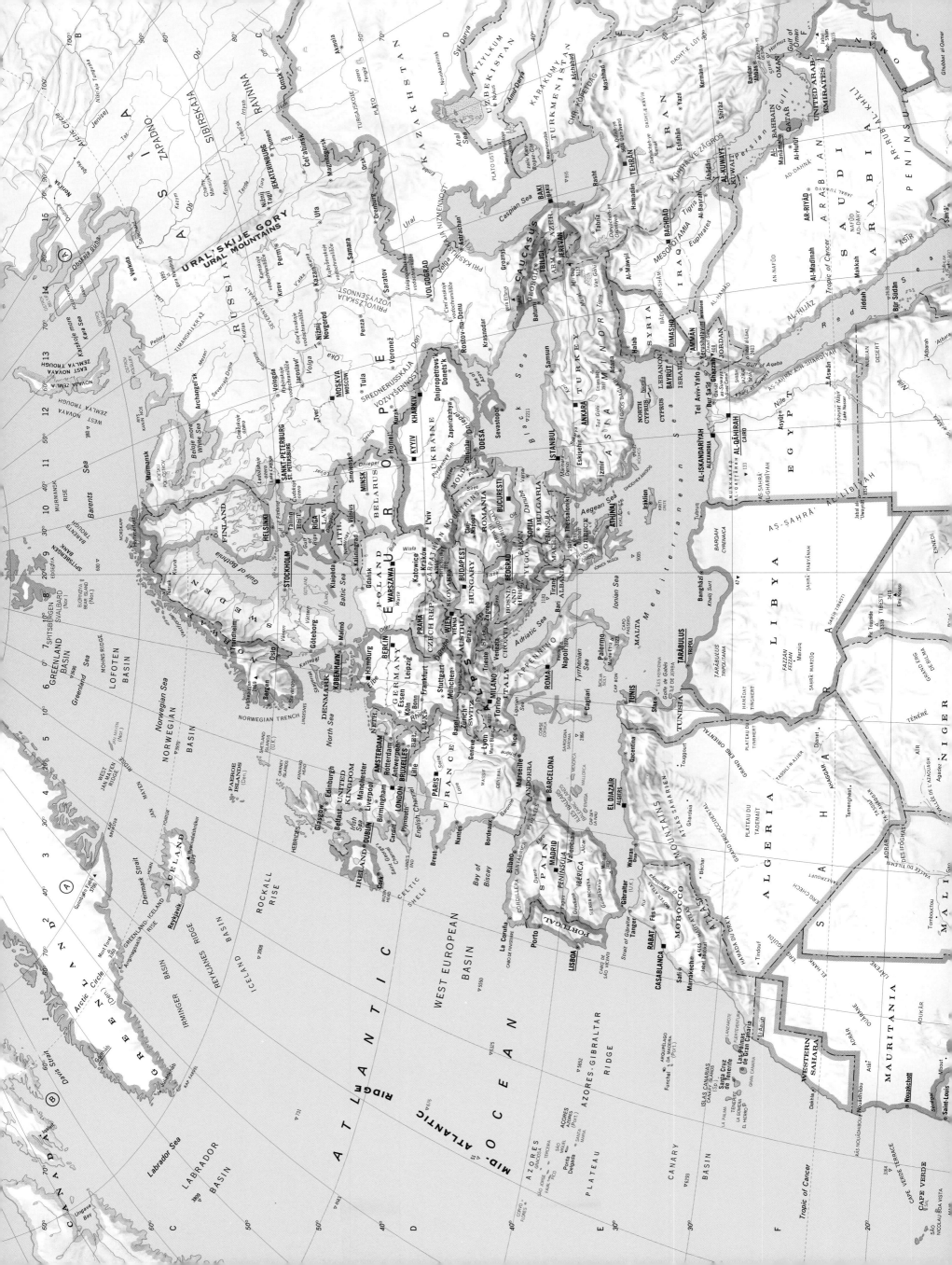

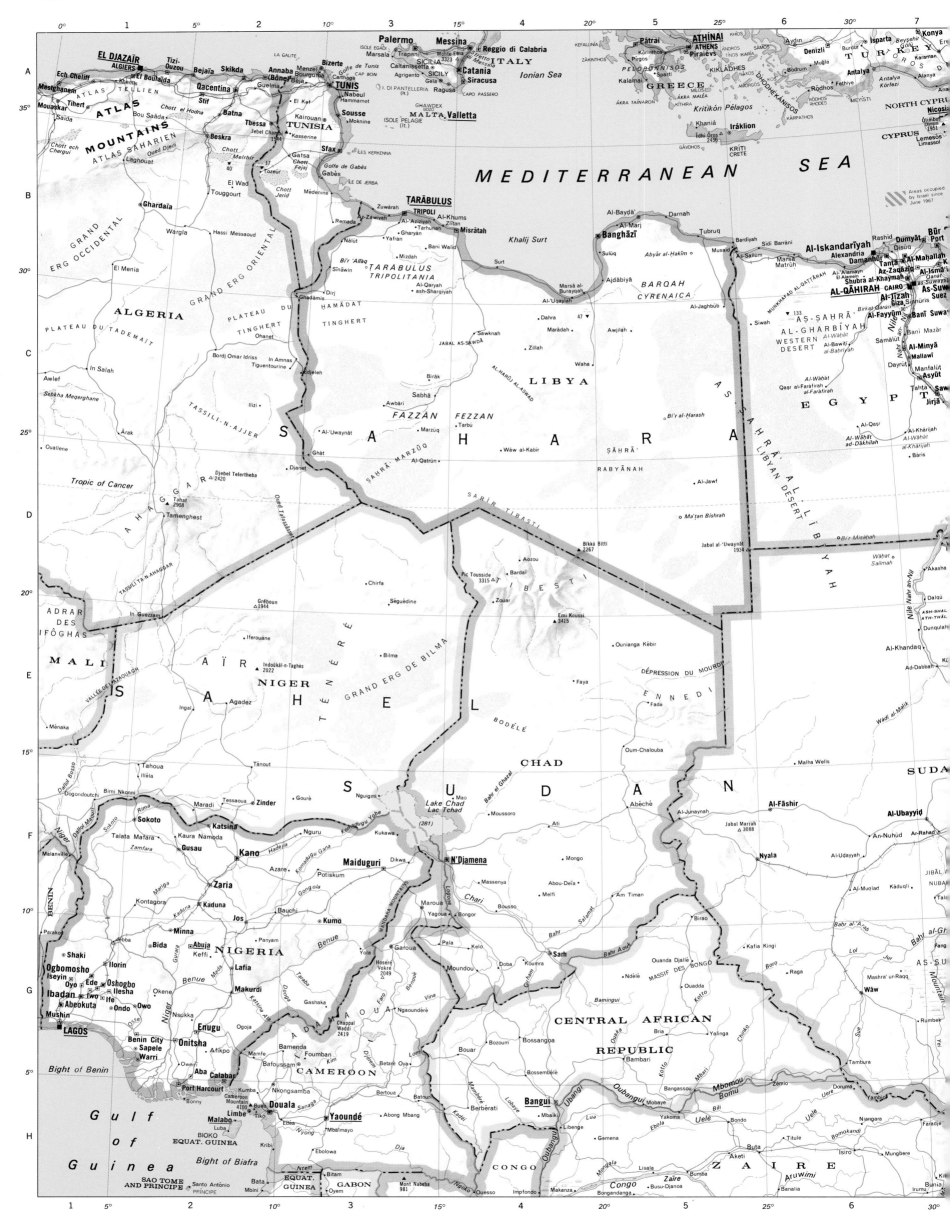

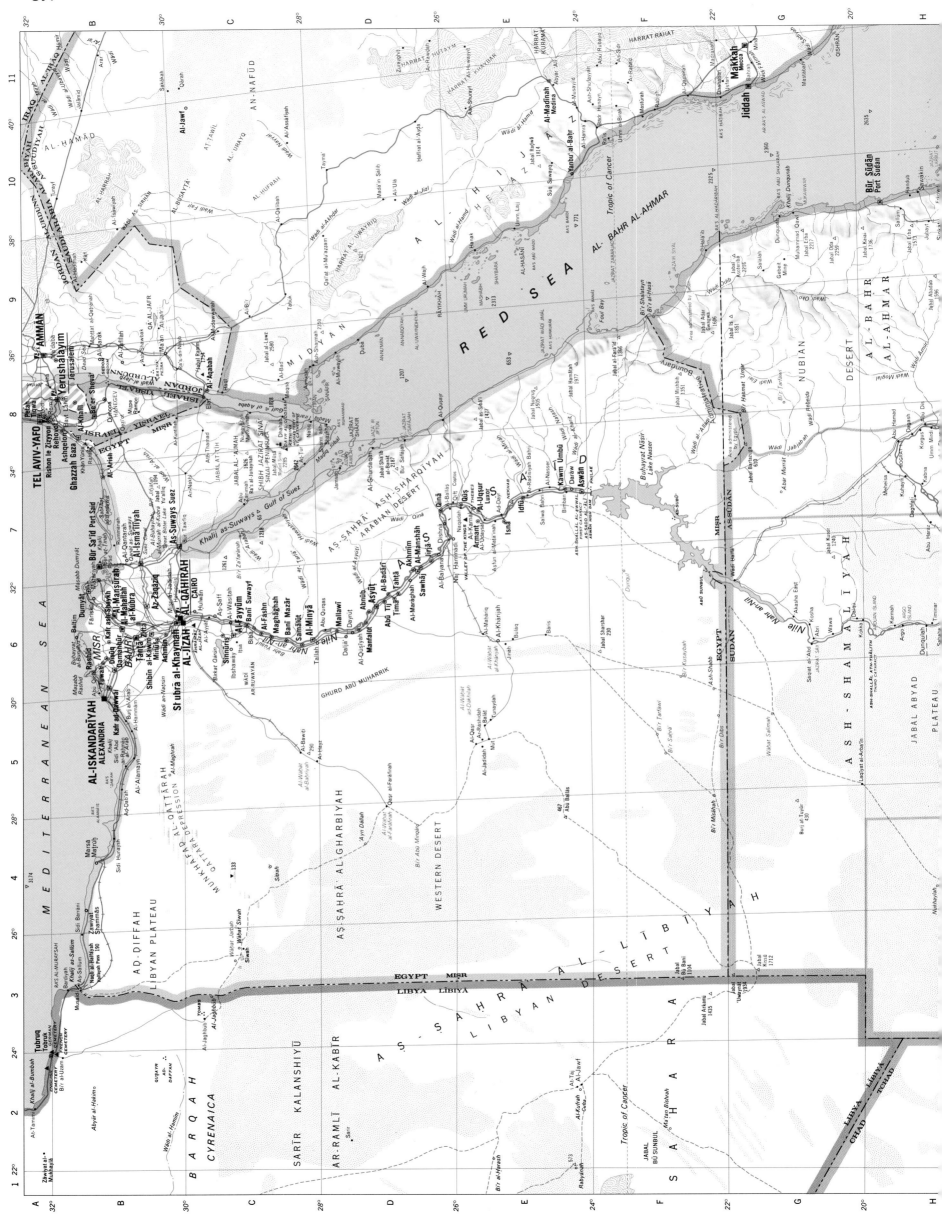

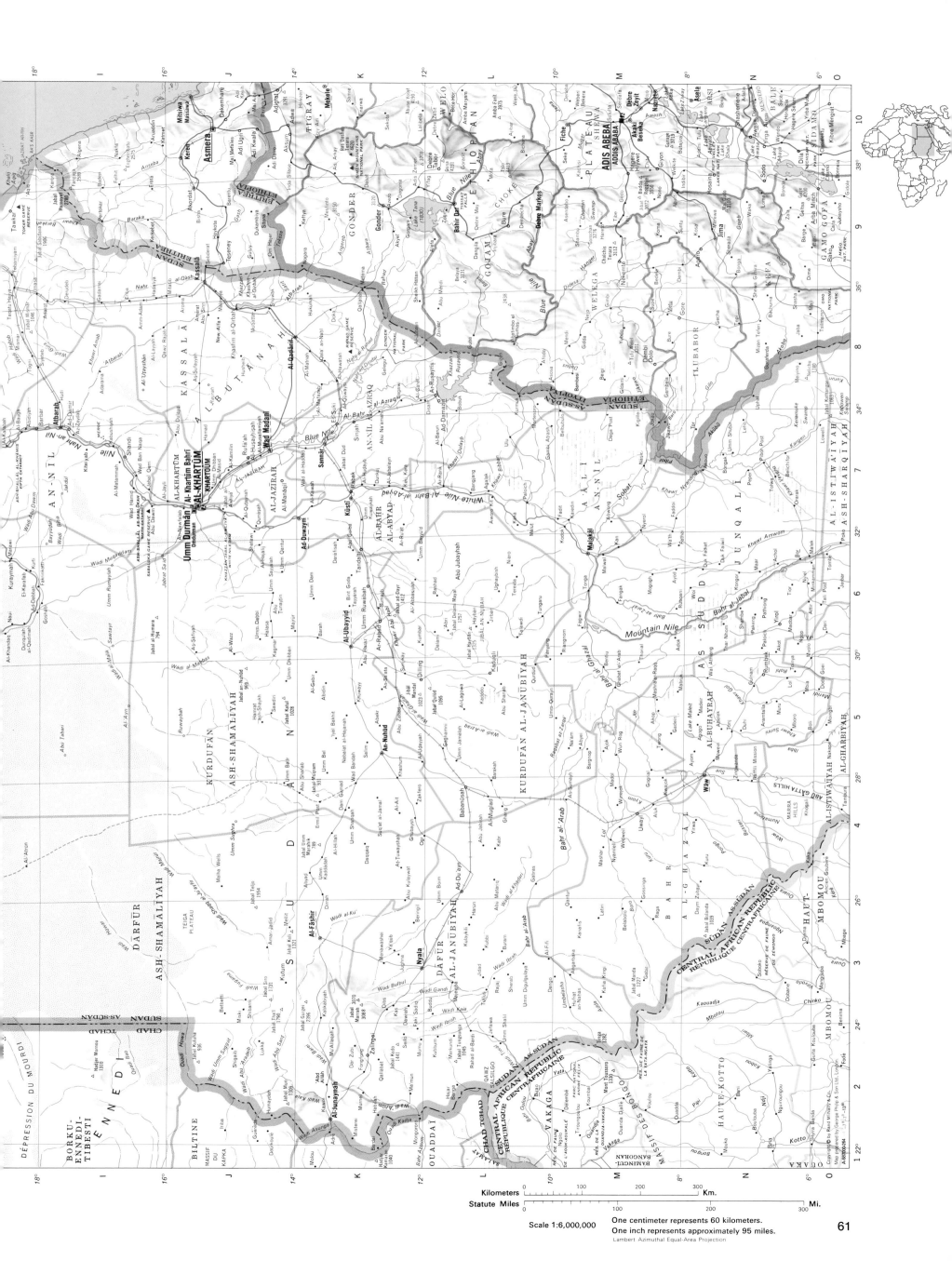

Kilometers
Statute Miles

Scale 1:6,000,000 One centimeter represents 60 kilometers.
One inch represents approximately 95 miles.
Lambert Azimuthal Equal-Area Projection

61

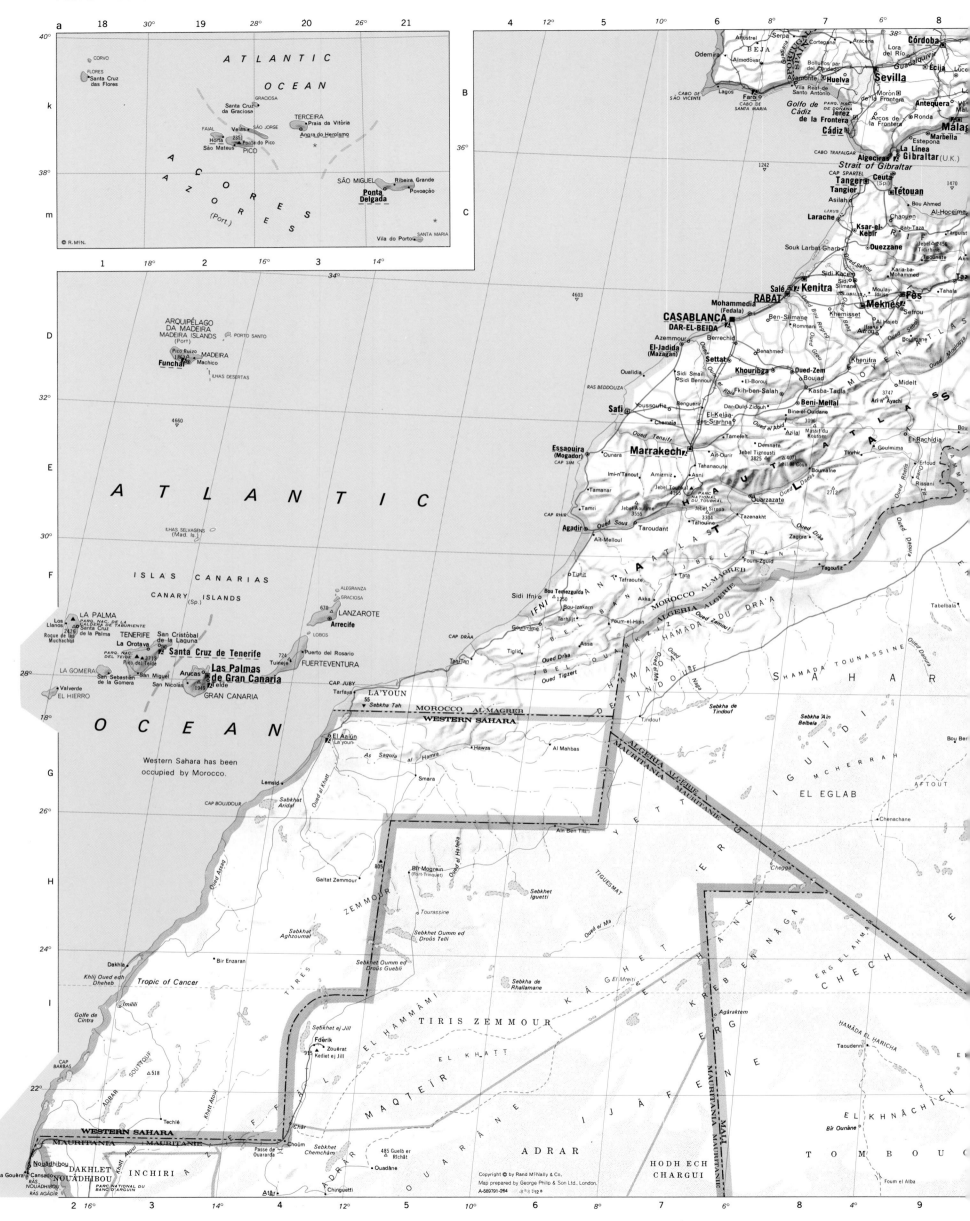

Western Sahara has been occupied by Morocco.

Copyright © by Rand McNally & Co.
Map prepared by George Philip & Son Ltd., London.
A-589791-264

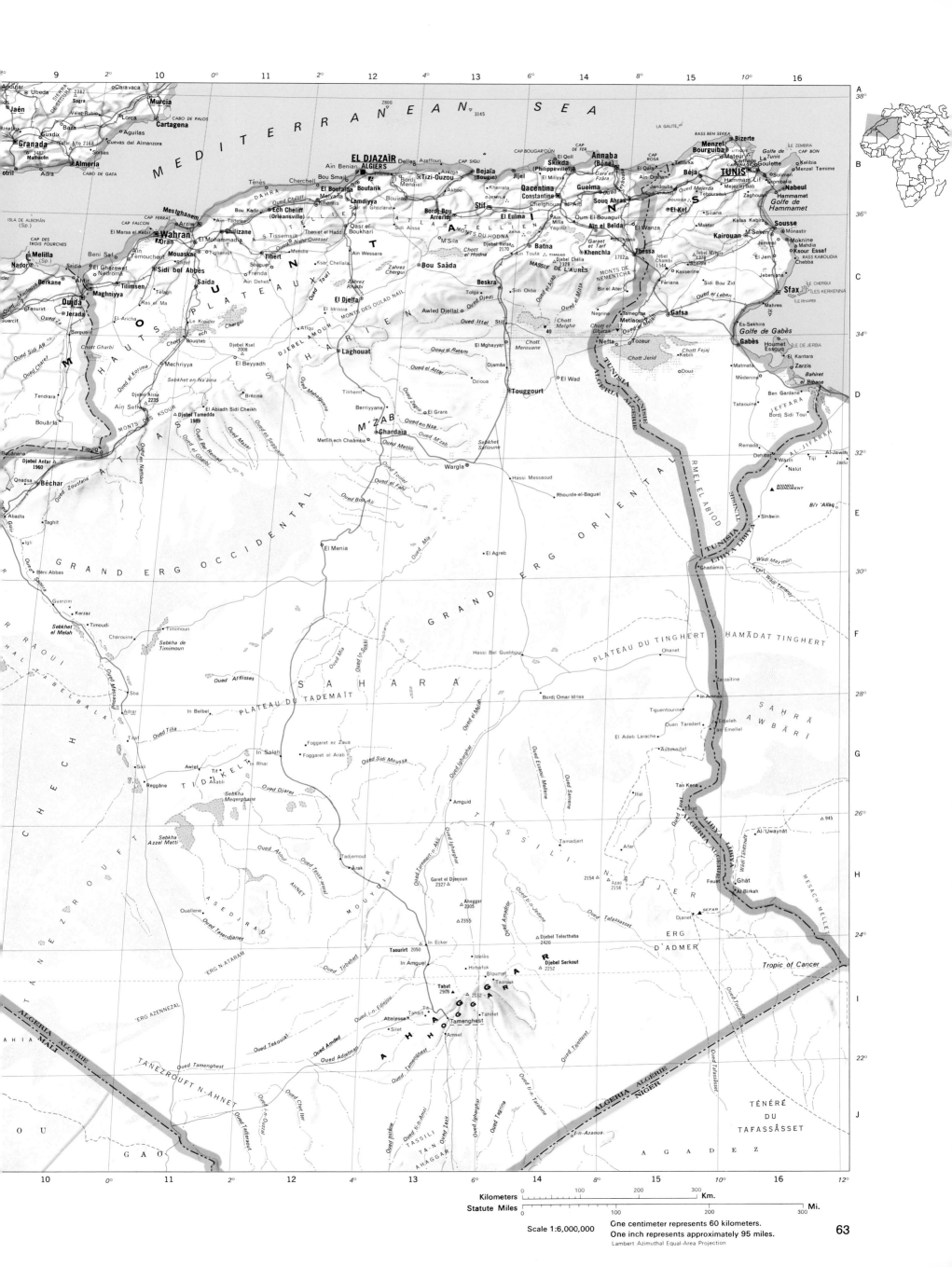

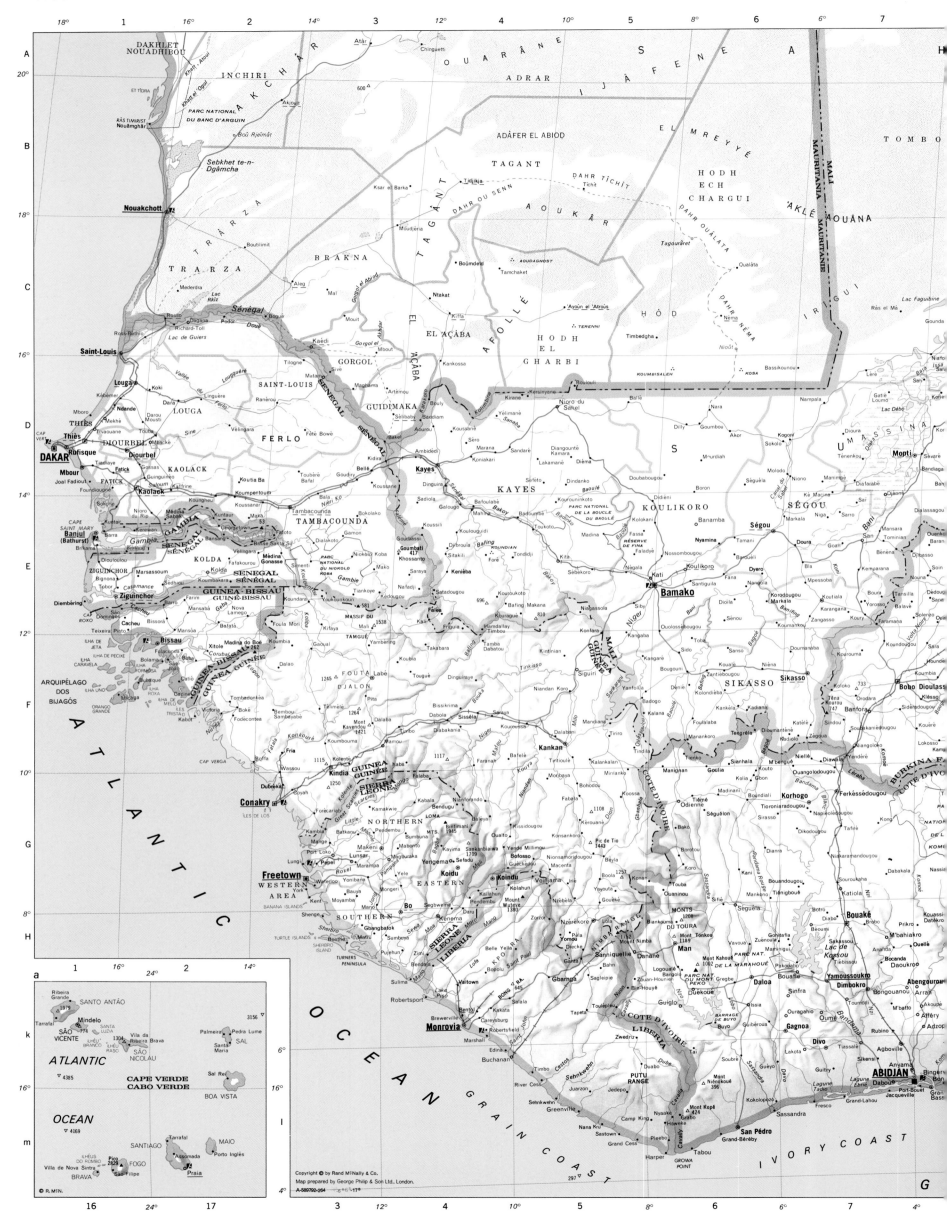

Kilometers 0 100 200 300 Km.

Statute Miles 0 100 200 300 Mi.

Scale 1:6,000,000   One centimeter represents 60 kilometers.
One inch represents approximately 95 miles.
Lambert Azimuthal Equal-Area Projection

Copyright © by Rand McNally & Co.
Map prepared by George Philip & Son Ltd., London.
A-589292-264

Kilometers
Statute Miles

Scale 1:6,000,000
One centimeter represents 60 kilometers.
One inch represents approximately 95 miles.
Lambert Azimuthal Equal-Area Projection

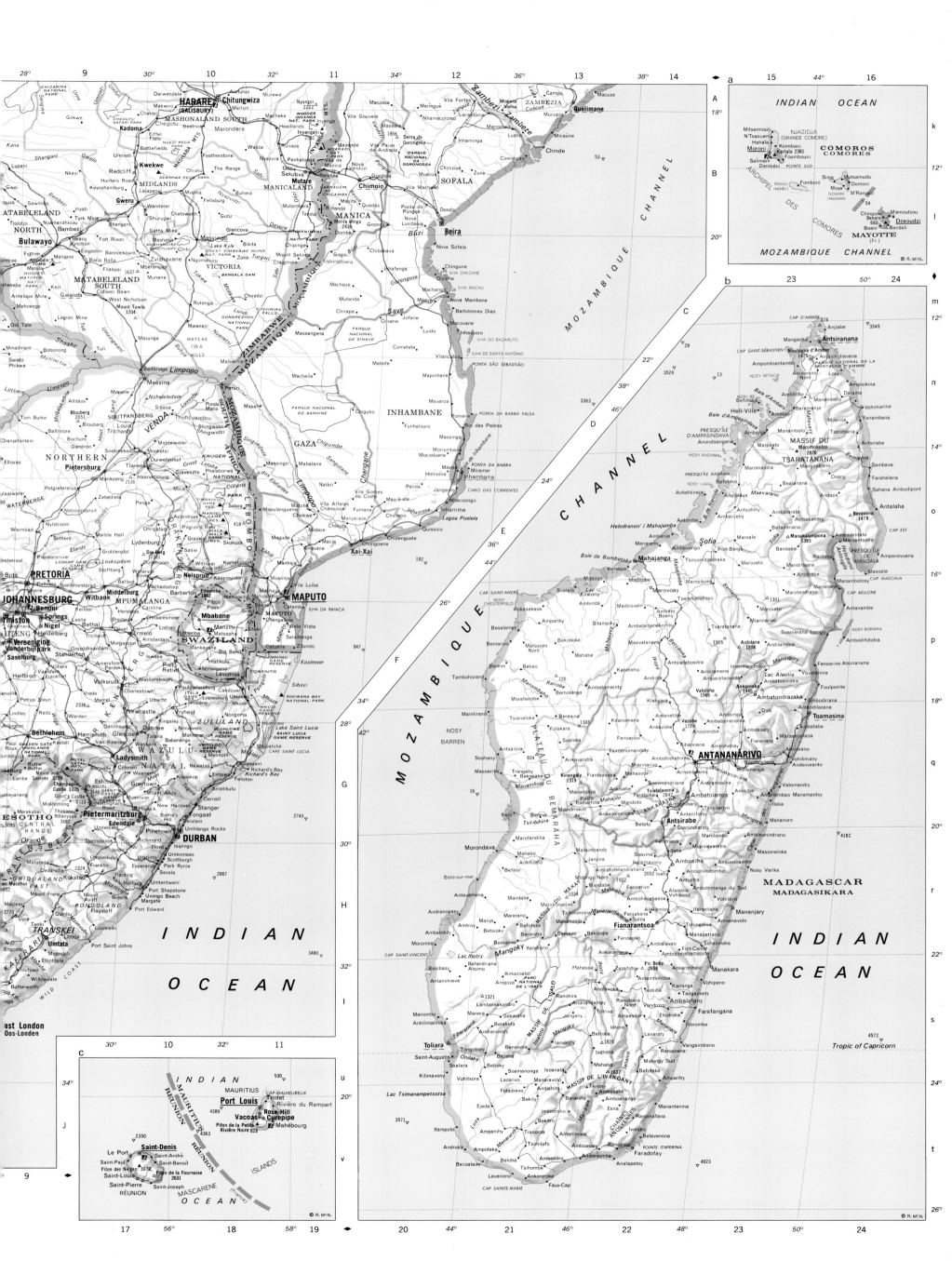

Australia

Inset map (top left)

PACIFIC OCEAN

PULAU WAIGEO
SELAT DAMPIER Equator
PULAU NUMFOOR KEPULAUAN SCHOUTEN
BIAK
SALAWATI Sorong Manokwari TANJUNG D'URVILLE
JAZIRAH DOBERAI NINIGO GROUP HERMIT ISLANDS MUSSAU ISLAND
PULAU MISOOL Teluk Berau Teluk Cenderawasih PEGUNUNGAN VAN REES ADMIRALTY ISLANDS
SERAM Bula Fakfak Memberamo Jayapura (Sukarnapura) MANUS ISLAND NEW HANOVER EMIRAU ISLAND
KEPULAUAN BANDA Kaimana PEGUNUNGAN MAOKE Aitape Wewak Kavieng NEW IRELAND Namatanai Rabaul Kokopo
INDONESIA Puncak Jaya 5030m Puncak Trikora 4750m Sepik BISMARCK ARCHIPELAGO KARKAR ISLAND Talasea
KAI KECIL PULAU WOKAM Dobo NEW GUINEA Madang UMBOI ISLAND Mount Ulawun 2334m
KEPULAUAN KAI PULAU KOBROOR Mt. Giluwe 4368m PAPUA Mt. Wilhelm 4509m NEW BRITAIN
KEPULAUAN YAMDENA PULAU TRANGAN NEW GUINEA Lae Huon Gulf Morobe
PULAU SELARU TANJUNG VALS Merauke Gulf of Papua Popondetta KIRIWINA ISLANDS
MELVILLE ISLAND COBURG PEN. CROKER ISLAND PULAU YOS SUDARSO Torres Strait CAPE YORK MOA ISLAND D'ENTRECASTEAUX ISLANDS
BATHURST ISLAND Van Diemen Gulf Arafura Sea GREAT BARRIER REEF MUYUA ISLAND Samarai
Darwin WESSEL ISLANDS Gulf of Carpentaria CAPE YORK PEN. Coral Sea
AUSTRALIA Port Moresby © 1979 R.M &N.
A-592200-264-1-1-1-2

Km. 0 100 200 300
Mi. 0 100 200

Main map

INDIAN OCEAN

Laut Sawu Savu Sea TIMOR Soe
Timor Sea Kupang
PULAU SEMAU PULAU ROTI
Ara

HIBERNIA REEF
ASHMORE ISLANDS CARTIER ISLAND (Austl.)
BROWSE ISLAND BONAPARTE ARCHIPELAGO CAPE LONDONDERRY CAPE CROKER
ADÈLE ISLAND Admiralty Gulf York Sound Joseph Bonaparte Gulf MELVILLE ISLAND BATHURST ISLAND Van Diemen Gulf Darwin Humpty Doo Jabiru
BUCCANEER ARCHIPELAGO BEAGLE REEF King Sound Queens Channel POINT BLAZE Rum Jungle Pine Creek ARNHEM LA
Cape Leveque KIMBERLEY PLATEAU Wyndham Ord Kununurra Katherine
Derby KING LEOPOLD RANGES Mount Ord 937 DURACK RANGES Lake Argyle Victoria Daly Waters
Broome Fitzroy Fitzroy Crossing Halls Creek Drysdale River Downs Wave Hill Newcastle Waters Lake Woods
ROWLEY SHOALS Victoria
CAPE LATOUCHE TREVILLE La Grange NORTHER
EIGHTY MILE BEACH TANAMI NORTHERN
C Lake Gregory DESERT TERRITOR
GREAT SANDY DESERT Lake White Barrow C
Port Hedland Goldsworthy Shay Gap Lake Wills
MONTE BELLO ISLANDS DAMPIER ARCHIPELAGO Dampier Roebourne De Grey Lake Dora Lake Auld Lake Mackay Mount Leisler 897 Mount Liebig 1524 Mount Zeil 1511 Al Sprin
BARROW ISLAND Karratha Marble Bar MACDONNELL RANGES
MUIRON ISLANDS Fortescue Nullagine Lake Macdonald Lake Neale
NORTH WEST CAPE Onslow Pannawonica Wittenoom HAMERSLEY RANGE Lake Disappointment
Exmouth Mount Brockman 1132 Mount Bruce 1235 Lake Amadeus
Exmouth Gulf Tom Price Mount Meharry 1251 WESTERN GIBSON DESERT Mount Olga 1069 Lake Amadeus
POINT CLOATES Ashburton Paraburdoo Newman Savory Ayers Rock 867 Mount Cockburn 1138 Mount Woodruffe 1440
CAPE CUVIER 1105 Mount Augustus Lake Essendon 906 A U S T
Lake Macleod Lyons Mount Aloysius 1085
Geographe Channel Carnarvon Peak Hill Lake Carnegie Lake Gillen
BERNIER ISLAND Gascoyne ROBINSON RANGE Lake Macdonald
DORRE ISLAND Shark Bay Wooramel Lake Wells
Naturaliste Channel Denham Murchison Wiluna GREAT VICTORIA DESERT SOU
DIRK HARTOG ISLAND Meekatharra AUSTRALIA Lake Maurice
STEEP POINT Nannine Lake Mingwal Maralinga
Kalbarri Cue Lake Austin Agnew Mount Redcliffe 562 Ooldea
Mount Magnet Sandstone Leonora Laverton SAINT PETER ISLAND
Northampton Yalgoo Lake Ballard Lake Carey CAPE ADIEU Streaky
Mullewa Lake Barlee Malcolm Lake Raeside NULLARBOR PLAIN Eyre
HOUTMAN ABROLHOS Pindar Menzies Zanthus Rawlinna Forrest Deakin Cape Arid
Geraldton Mongers Lake Kalgoorlie-Boulder Haig Eucla INVESTIG
Dongara Three Springs Lake Moore Coolgardie Southern Cross Lake Lefroy Great Australian Bight
GREEN HEAD Dalwallinu Bonnie Rock Lake Cowan CAPE ADIEU
Mooral Bencubbin Bullfinch Norseman Lake Dundas POINT CULVER
Wanneroo Northam Merredin Southern Cross Lake Johnston
Perth York Kellerberrin Ravensthorpe CAPE ARID
Fremantle DARLING RANGE Beverley Brookton Hyden Esperance ARCHIPELAGO OF THE RECHERCHE
Pinjarra Narrogin Newdegate Hopetoun Esperance Bay
Bunbury Wagin Nyabing Gnowangerup
Geographe Bay Collie Katanning CAPE ADIEU
CAPE NATURALISTE Busselton Bridgetown Bluff Knoll 1096 Great Australian Bight
Augusta Manjimup Mount Barker
CAPE LEEUWIN Pemberton Albany CAPE VANCOUVER
POINT D'ENTRECASTEAUX WEST CAPE HOWE King George Sound

SOUTHERN OCE

Tropic of Capricorn

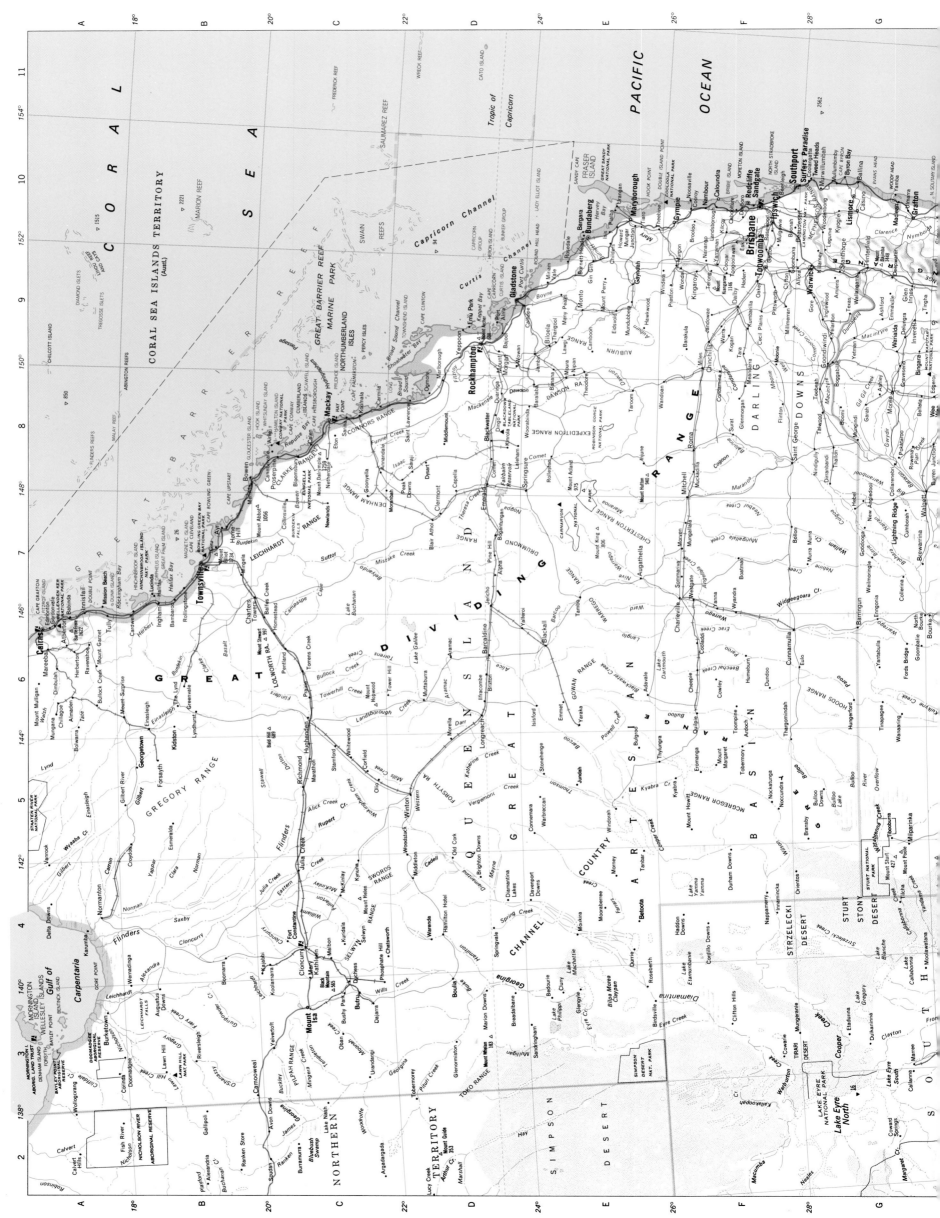

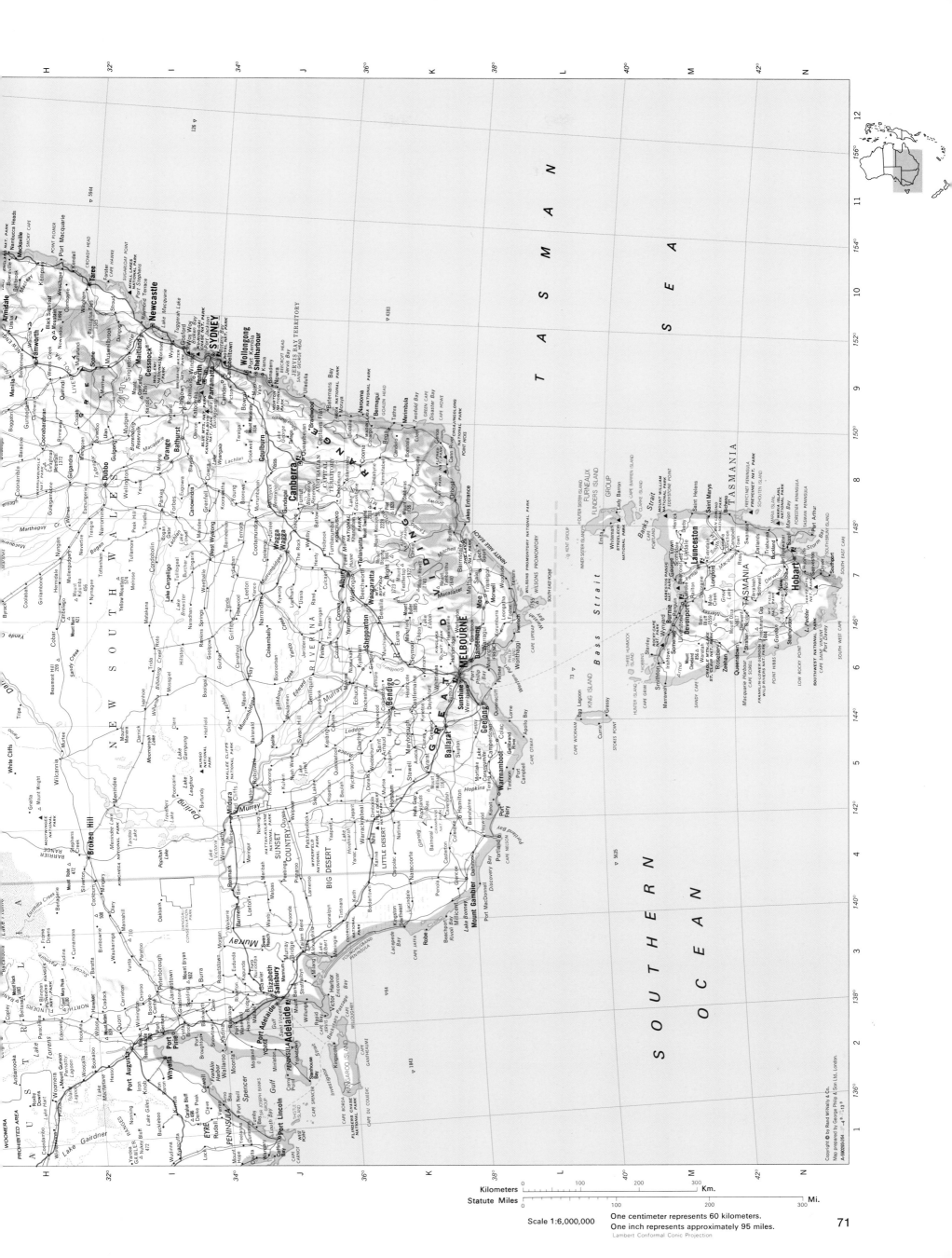

Kilometers
Statute Miles

Scale 1:6,000,000

One centimeter represents 60 kilometers.
One inch represents approximately 95 miles.

Lambert Conformal Conic Projection

New Zealand

Whangarei
Dargaville
CAPE REINGA
NORTH CAPE
Bargaungu Bay
Doubtless Bay
CAPE BRETT
Ahipara Bay
TAUROA POINT
Okaihau
Opua
Wellsford
Bream Bay
GREAT BARRIER ISLAND
Kaipara Harbour
Hauraki Gulf
Takapuna
Devonport
COROMANDEL PENINSULA
Auckland
Manukau Harbour
Pukekohe
Thames
Waiuku
Waihi
Huntly
Morrinsville
Bay of Plenty
CAPE RUNAWAY
EAST CAPE
Hamilton
Cambridge
Tauranga
Te Awamutu
Whakatane
Opotiki
Te Kuiti
Tokoroa
Rotorua
Murapara
North Taranaki Bight
Taupo
Lake Taupo
Gisborne
Waitara
Taumarunui
Tarawera
Wairoa
New Plymouth
Mt Egmont 2518
Hawke Bay
MAHIA PENINSULA
Opunake
Stratford
Ruapehu 797
Napier
South Taranaki Bight
Hawera
Raethi
CAPE KIDNAPPERS
Hastings
Patea
Taihape
Waipukurau
Wanganui
Dannevirke
Palmerston North
Woodville
CAPE FAREWELL
Golden Bay
Levin
D'URVILLE ISLAND
Otaki
Hector 1529
Masterton
Takaka
Tasman Bay
Cook Strait
Lake Wairarapa
Motueka
Lower Hutt
Karamea Bight
Nelson
Picton
Wellington
Seddonville
Richmond
CAPE PALLISER
1875 Mount Owen
Blenheim
Westport
Wairau
CAPE FOULWIND
Butler
Mt. Uriah 1501
Tapuaenuku 2885
CAPE CAMPBELL
Reefton
2337 Mount Travers
Manakau 2610
Runanga
Kaikoura
Greymouth
Waiau
Hokitika
Ross
Waipara
Mount Murchison 2400
Oxford
Whataroa
Pegasus Bay
Sheffield
Kaiapoi
Mount Cook 3754
Methven
Christchurch
Lake Tekapo
Mount Somers
Little River
CASCADE POINT
BANKS PENINSULA
Haast
Southbridge
Ashburton
Lake Pukaki
Fairlie
Mount Aspiring 3035
Lake Hawea
Canterbury Bight
Omarama
Timaru
2756 Mount Tutoko
Wanaka
Mount Saint Bathans 2086
Kurow
Waitaki
Waimate
LIVINGSTONE MTS
Queenstown
Cromwell
Ranfurly
Oamaru
Doubtful Sound
Lake Te Anau
Lake Wakatipu
Alexandra
Palmerston
RESOLUTION ISLAND
Te Anau
Kingston
Roxburgh
Beaumont
Port Chalmers
CAPE PROVIDENCE
Mossburn
Edievale
Dunedin
Nightcaps
Winton
Gore
Milton
Otautau
STEWART ISLAND
Te Waewae Bay
Riverton
Kaitangata
Invercargill
Tokanui
Tahakopa
Foveaux Strait
Bluff
Mt Anglem 978
SOUTHERN ALPS

Copyright © by Rand McNally & Co.
A-591600-286

Scale 1:6,000,000
One centimeter represents 60 kilometers.
One inch represents approximately 95 miles.
Lambert Conformal Conic Projection

Kilometers 0 100 200 300 Km.
Statute Miles 0 100 200 300 Mi.

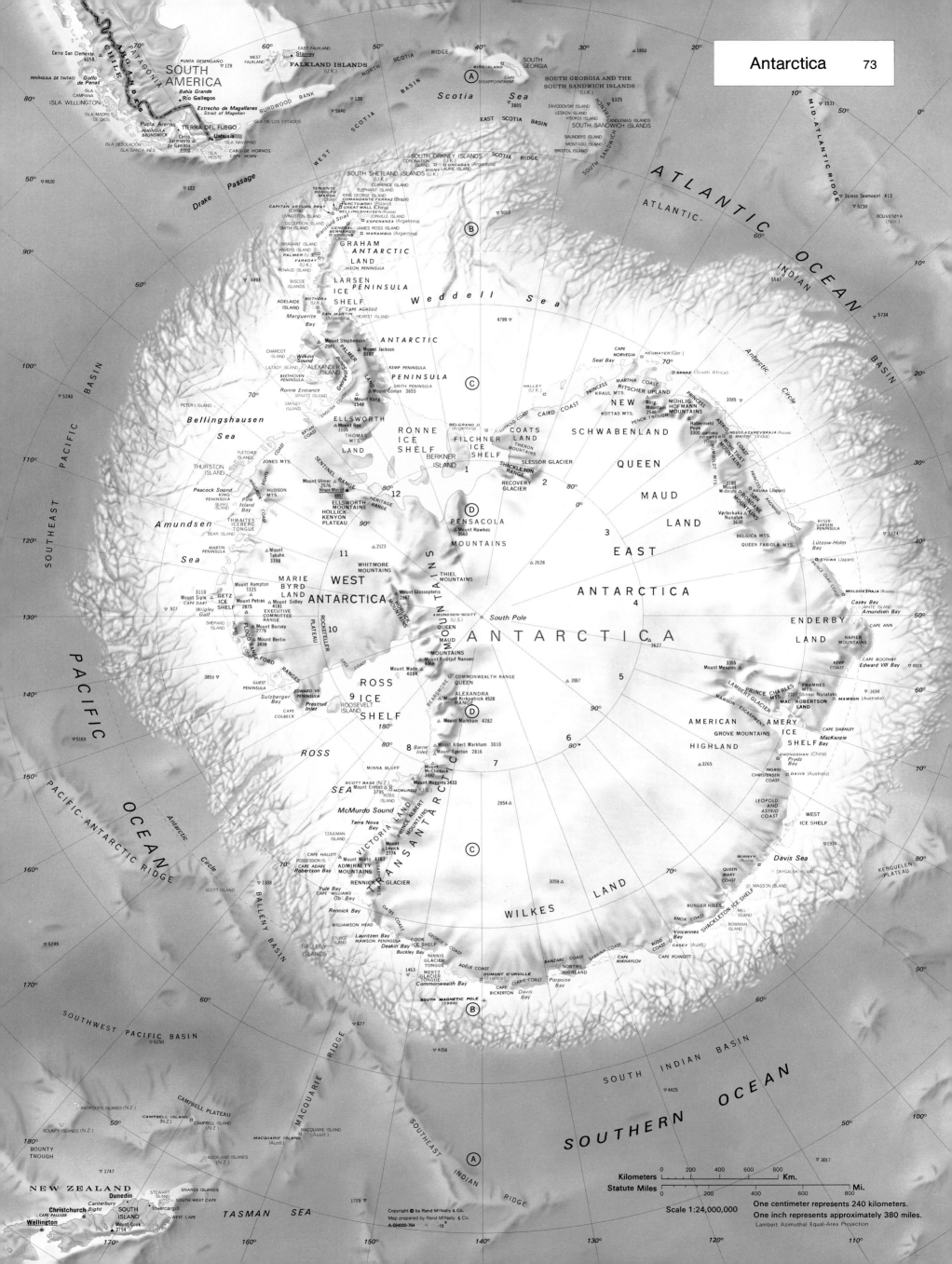

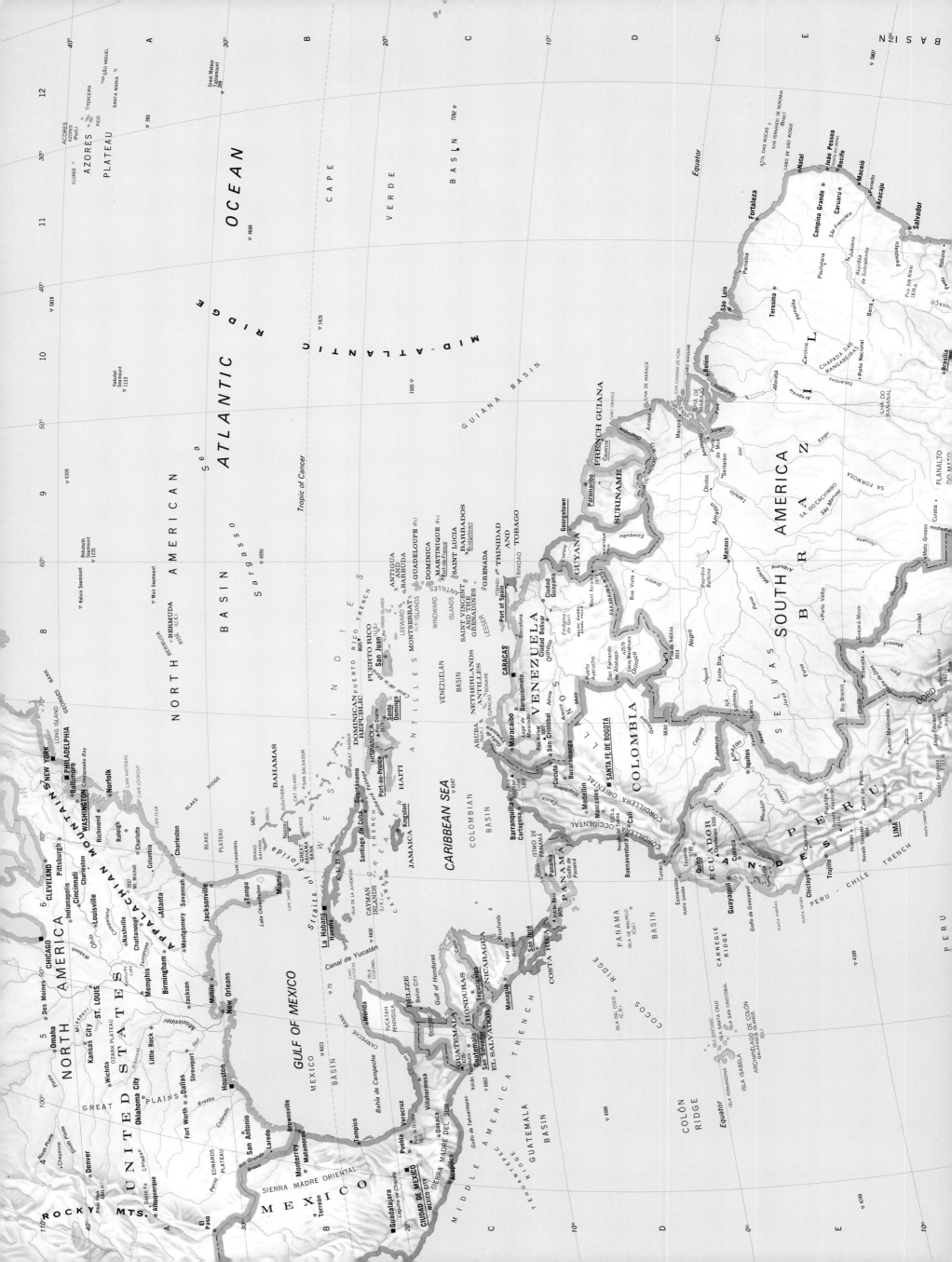

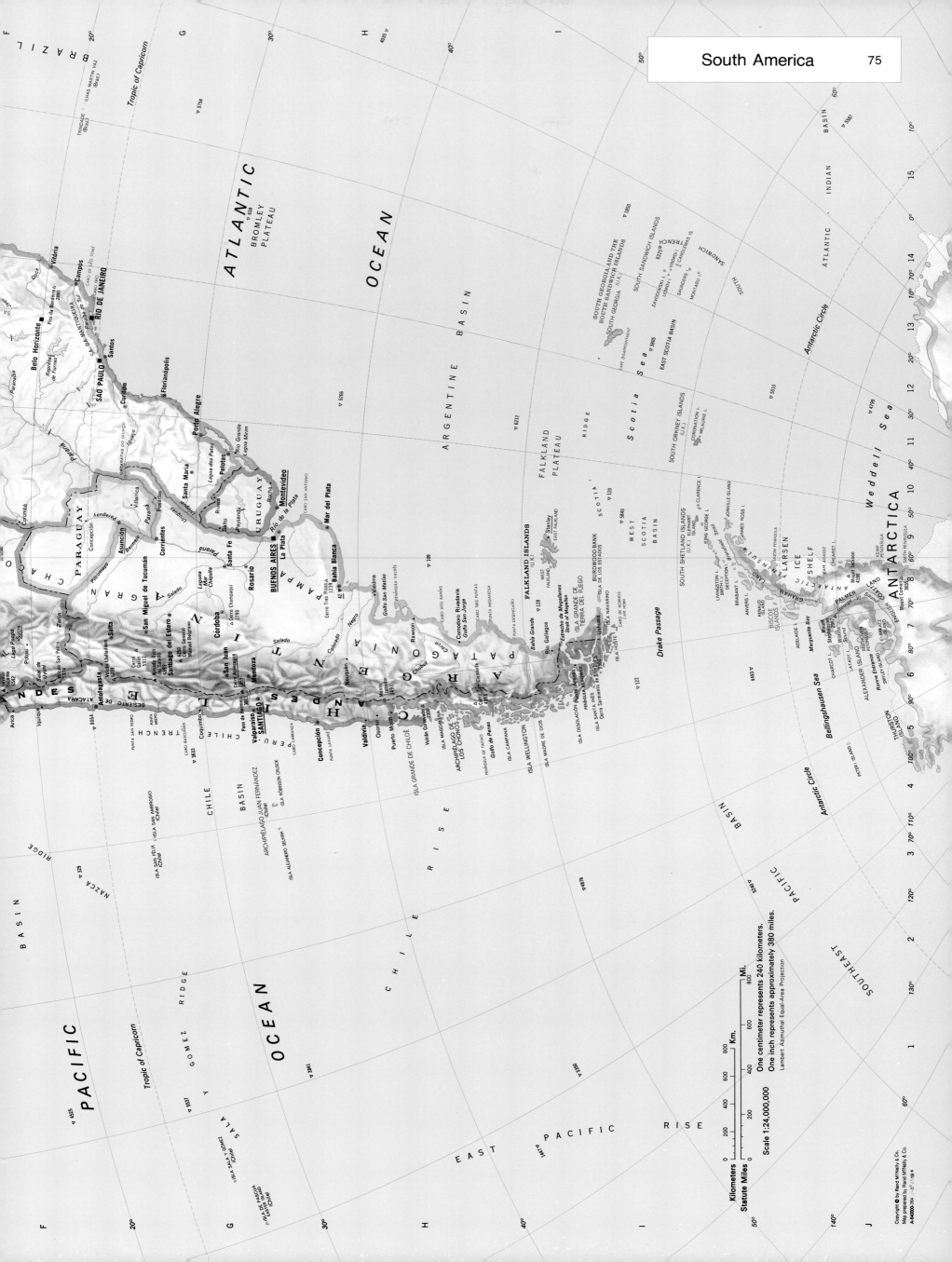

F   BRAZIL   20°   G   30°   H   △4035   40°   I   50°

Tropic of Capricorn

ILHAS MARTIM VAZ
(Braz.)

TRINDADE
(Braz.)

▽658   BROMLEY
PLATEAU

ATLANTIC

Vitória

Campos

CABO DE SÃO TOMÉ

RIO DE JANEIRO

△ Pico da Bandeira
2890

SA. DA MANTIQUEIRA

▽5754

Belo Horizonte

Represa
de Furnas

Paraíba

Santos

SÃO PAULO

Curitiba

Florianópolis

OCEAN

CATARATAS DO IGUAÇU

Iguaçu

Porto Alegre

ARGENTINE   BASIN

Paraná

CHACO

PARAGUAY

Kembela

Concepción

Asunción

Paraná

Corrientes

Santa Maria

Villarrica

Pilcomayo

Picada

Pelotas

Rio Grande

Lagoa dos Patos

Santa Fe

URUGUAY

Salto

Rivera

Uruguay

Paysandú

Lagoa Mirim

Rocha

Montevideo

RIO SAN ANTONIO

Río de la Plata

▽5266

▽6212

FALKLAND   PLATEAU

RIDGE

SOUTH GEORGIA AND THE
SOUTH SANDWICH ISLANDS

SOUTH GEORGIA
(U.K.)

▽8329

SOUTH SANDWICH ISLANDS

ZAVODOVSKI I.

LESKOV I.

VISOKOI I.

SAUNDERS I.

CANDLEMAS IS.

MONTAGU I.

▽1850

CAPE DISAPPOINTMENT

BRISTOL I.

SANDWICH

TRENCH

Antarctic Circle

ATLANTIC

INDIAN

BASIN

▽5507

15

14   10°

13   0°

▽4558

EAST SCOTIA BASIN

▽3805

Scotia   Sea

▽5010

SOUTH ORKNEY ISLANDS
(U.K.)

CORONATION I.

BEAUREPAIRE I.

Weddell   Sea

ANTARCTICA

60°

70°

PAMPA

GRAN

Laguna
Mar
Chiquita

San Miguel de Tucumán

Santiago del Estero

Córdoba

△Cerro Champaquí
2790

Rosario

La Plata

BUENOS AIRES

Bahía Blanca

42 ▽

▽109

Mar del Plata

Viedma

Negro

Colorado

Golfo San Matías

PENÍNSULA VALDÉS

Rawson

Golfo San Jorge

Comodoro Rivadavia

PUNTA MERCEDES

▽128

GRANDE DE
TIERRA DEL FUEGO

Río Gallegos

Bahía Grande

CABO SANTA INÉS

Cerro Sarmiento 2180

Ushuaia

CABO DOS BAHÍAS

CABO TRES PUNTAS

PUNTA DESENGAÑO

ISLA DE LOS ESTADOS

CABO SAN DIEGO

Estrecho de Magallanes
Strait of Magellan

CABO DE HORNOS
CABO HORN

ISLA NAVARINO

ISLA HOSTE

Drake   Passage

WEST   SCOTIA   BASIN

▽5840

▽120

SCOTIA

FALKLAND ISLANDS
(U.K.)

WEST
FALKLAND

EAST FALKLAND

Stanley

BURDWOOD BANK

▽122

SOUTH SHETLAND ISLANDS
(U.K.)

CLARENCE I.

ELEPHANT I.

KING GEORGE I.

JOINVILLE ISLAND

JAMES ROSS I.

LIVINGSTON I.

DECEPTION I.

SMITH I.

SNOW I.

BRABANT I.

ANVERS I.

BISCOE ISLANDS

ADELAIDE I.

Marguerite Bay

CHARCOT I.

LATADY I.

ALEXANDER ISLAND

PETER I ISLAND

Bellingshausen Sea

▽4493

Antarctic Circle

THURSTON
ISLAND

GRAHAM

PALMER

LARSEN

ICE

SHELF

PENINSULA

ANTARCTIC

Mount Jackson
4190

KEMP
PENINSULA

EDITH RONNE
LAND

Mount Owen 2367

Mount Stephenson

ROONE

Ronne Entrance

ANDES

Arica

Iquique

Antofagasta

Volcán Llullaillaco
6739

Cerro Galán
5912

Salta

Jujuy

Sucre

Lago Poopó

Potosí

Salar de Uyuni

ANDES

ATACAMA

DESIERTO DE

PUNTA MEDIO

San Juan

Mendoza

Cerro Aconcagua
6959

△ Cerro Mercedario
6770

Paso de Agua Negra

Valparaíso

SANTIAGO

Concepción

CHILE

PERU

TRENCH

Valdivia

Osorno

Puerto Montt

Volcán Corcovado
2300

Gulfo de Ancud

ISLA GRANDE DE CHILOÉ

ARCHIPIÉLAGO DE
LOS CHONOS

PENÍNSULA DE TAITAO

Golfo de Penas

ISLA CAMPANA

ISLA WELLINGTON

ISLA MADRE DE DIOS

ISLA SANTA INÉS

Monte Tronador
3491

PATAGONIA

ANDES

Neuquén

Salado

ARGENTINA

NAZCA

BASIN

▽329

▽3633

CHILE   BASIN

GOMEZ   RIDGE

ISLA SALA Y GÓMEZ
(Chile)

ISLA DE PASCUA
EASTER ISLAND
(Chile)

ISLA SAN FÉLIX
(Chile)

ISLA SAN AMBROSIO
(Chile)

ARCHIPIÉLAGO JUAN FERNÁNDEZ
(Chile)

ISLA ROBINSON CRUSOE

ISLA ALEJANDRO SELKIRK

PACIFIC

OCEAN

Tropic of Capricorn

▽4325

▽9537

▽3941

CHILE   RISE

▽4876

PACIFIC

BASIN

SOUTHEAST

PACIFIC   RISE

EAST   PACIFIC   RISE

F   20°   G   30°   H   40°   I   50°

Mi.   800

Km.   1000

600

800

400

600

200

400

200

Kilometers   0

Statute Miles   0

One centimeter represents 240 kilometers.
One inch represents approximately 380 miles.

Scale 1:24,000,000

Lambert Azimuthal Equal-Area Projection

Copyright © by Rand McNally & Co.
Map prepared by Esselte Map Service AB, Stockholm.
A-549100-264

Kilometers
Statute Miles

Scale 1:12,000,000
One centimeter represents 120 kilometers.
One inch represents approximately 190 miles.
Oblique Conic Conformal Projection

ATLANTIC

OCEAN

PACIFIC OCEAN

FALKLAND
ISLANDS
(U.K.)

Kilometers
Statute Miles

One centimeter represents 120 kilometers.
One inch represents approximately 190 miles.

Scale 1:12,000,000
Oblique Conic Conformal Projection

Copyright © by Rand McNally & Co.
Map prepared by Esselte Map Service AB, Stockholm.
A-549200-264

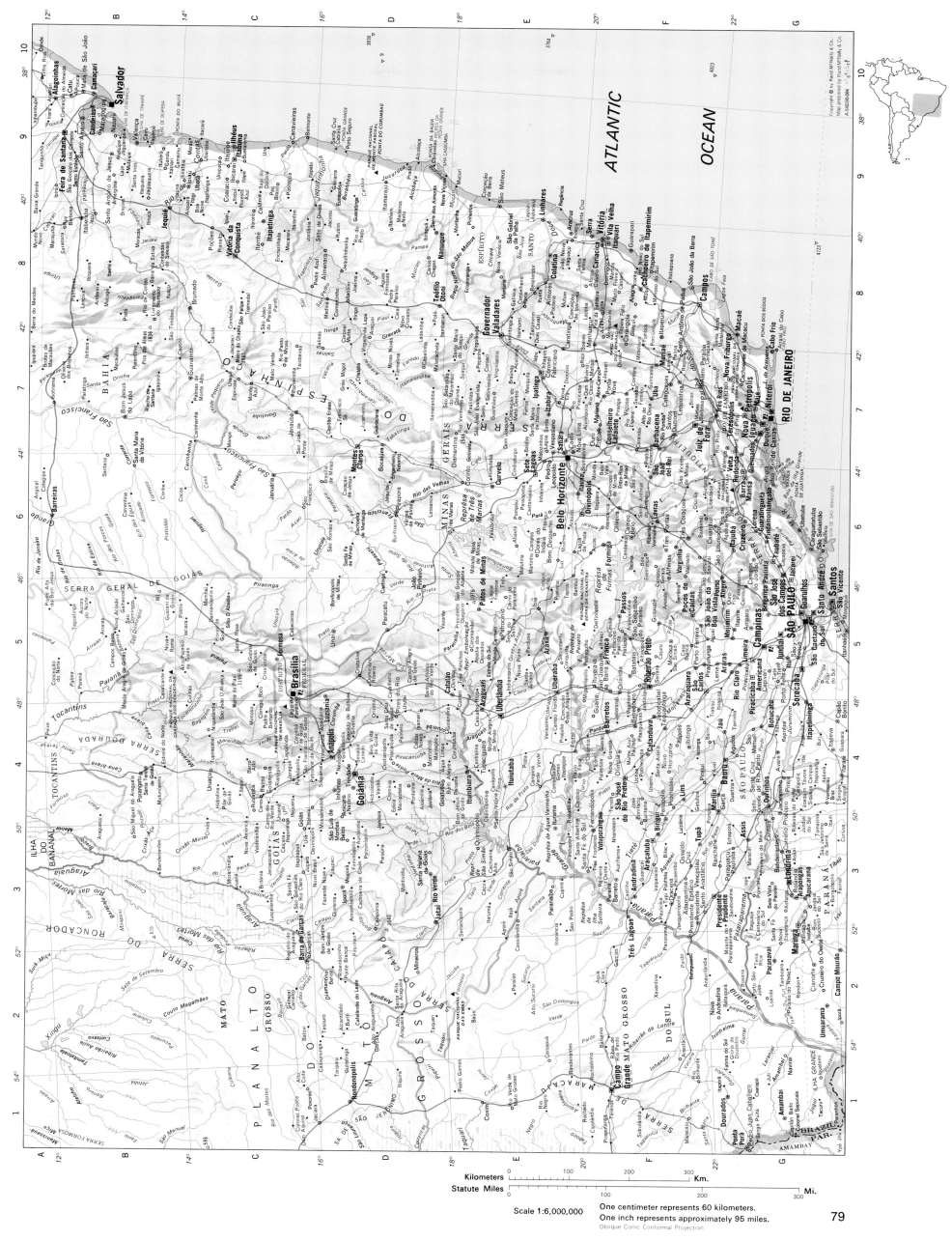

Kilometers
Statute Miles

Scale 1:6,000,000
One centimeter represents 60 kilometers.
One inch represents approximately 95 miles.
Oblique Conic Conformal Projection

79

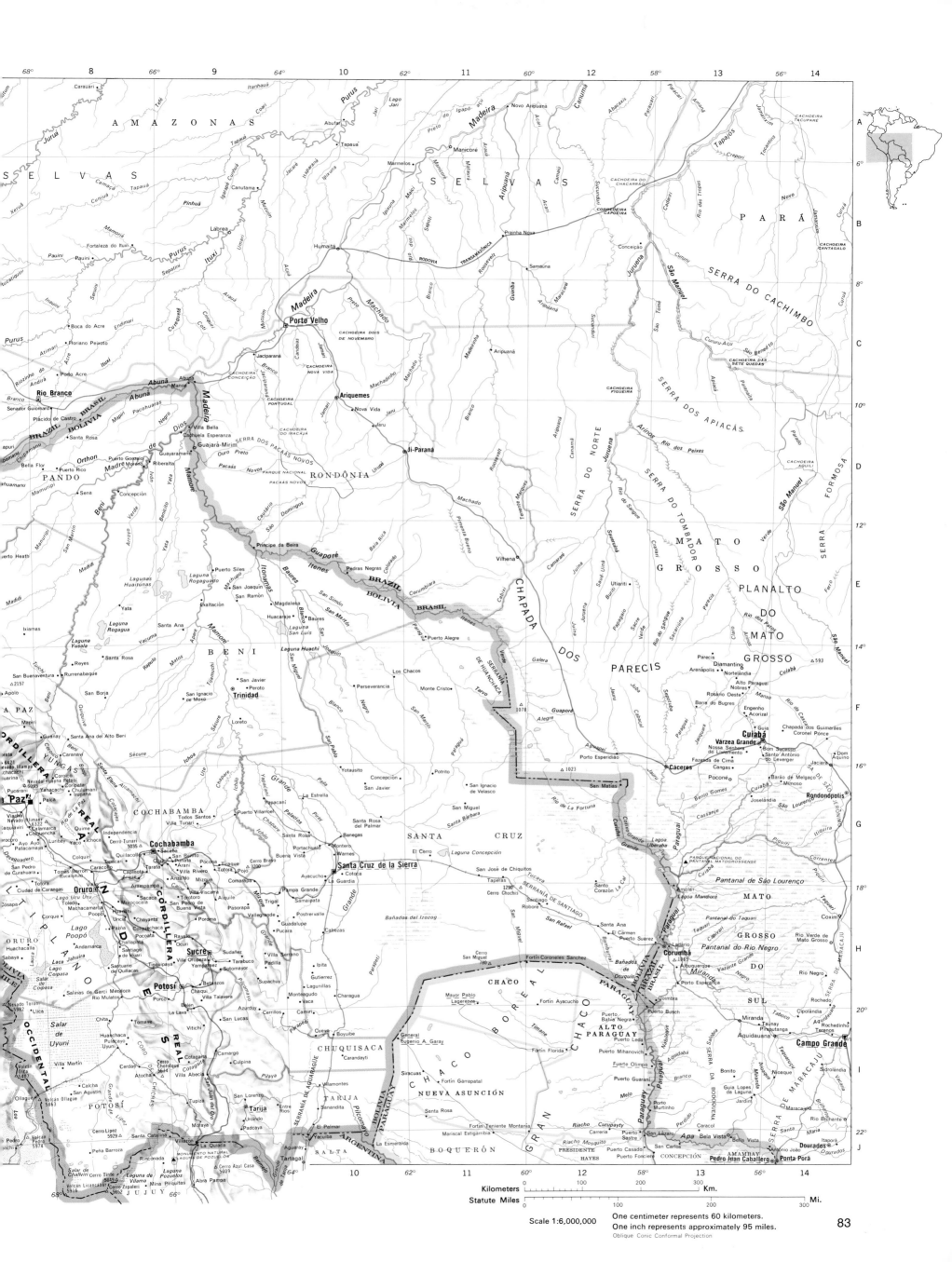

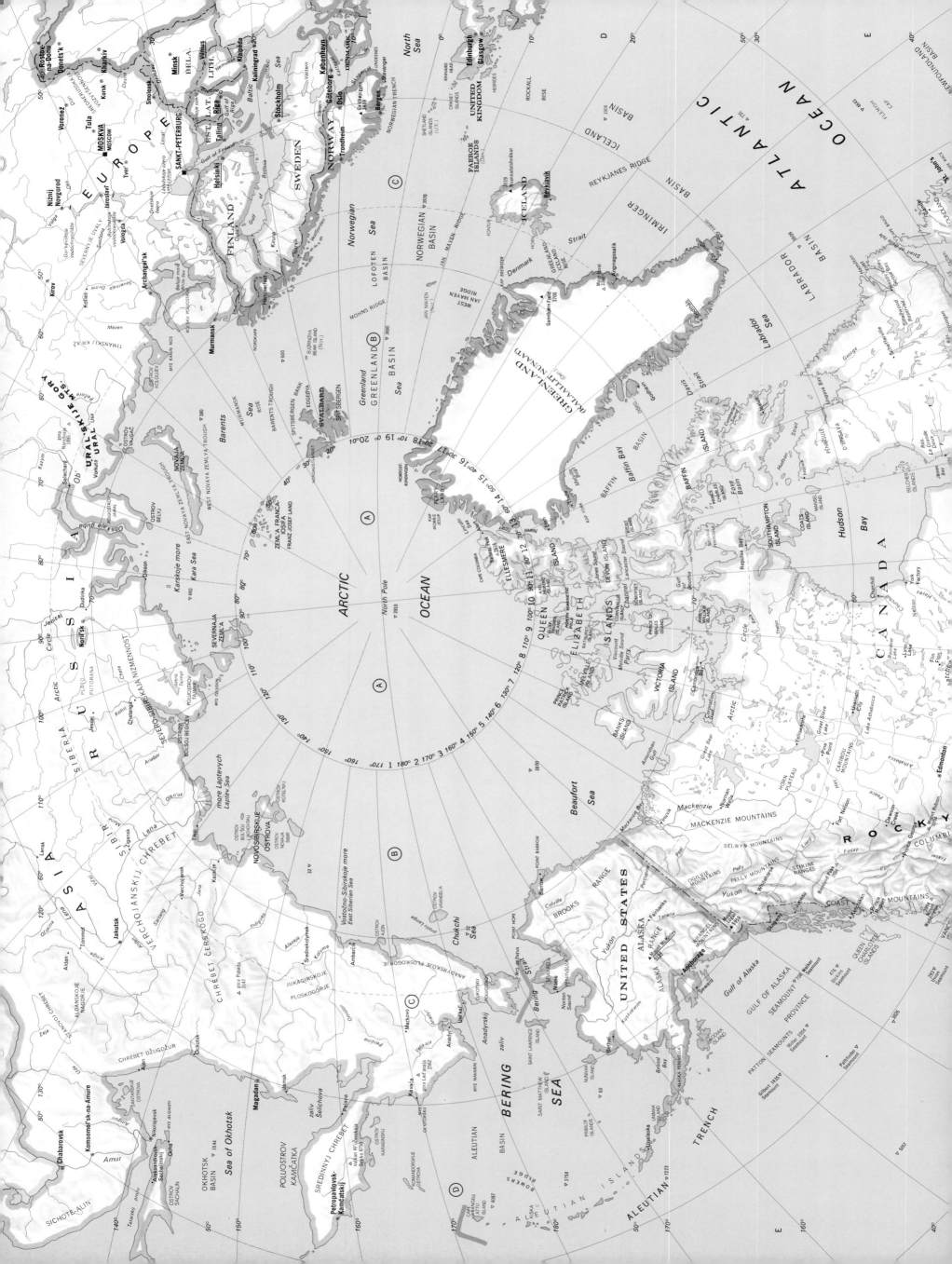

Mexico

Kilometers
Statute Miles

Scale 1:6,000,000

One centimeter represents 60 kilometers.
One inch represents approximately 95 miles.

Lambert Conformal Conic Projection

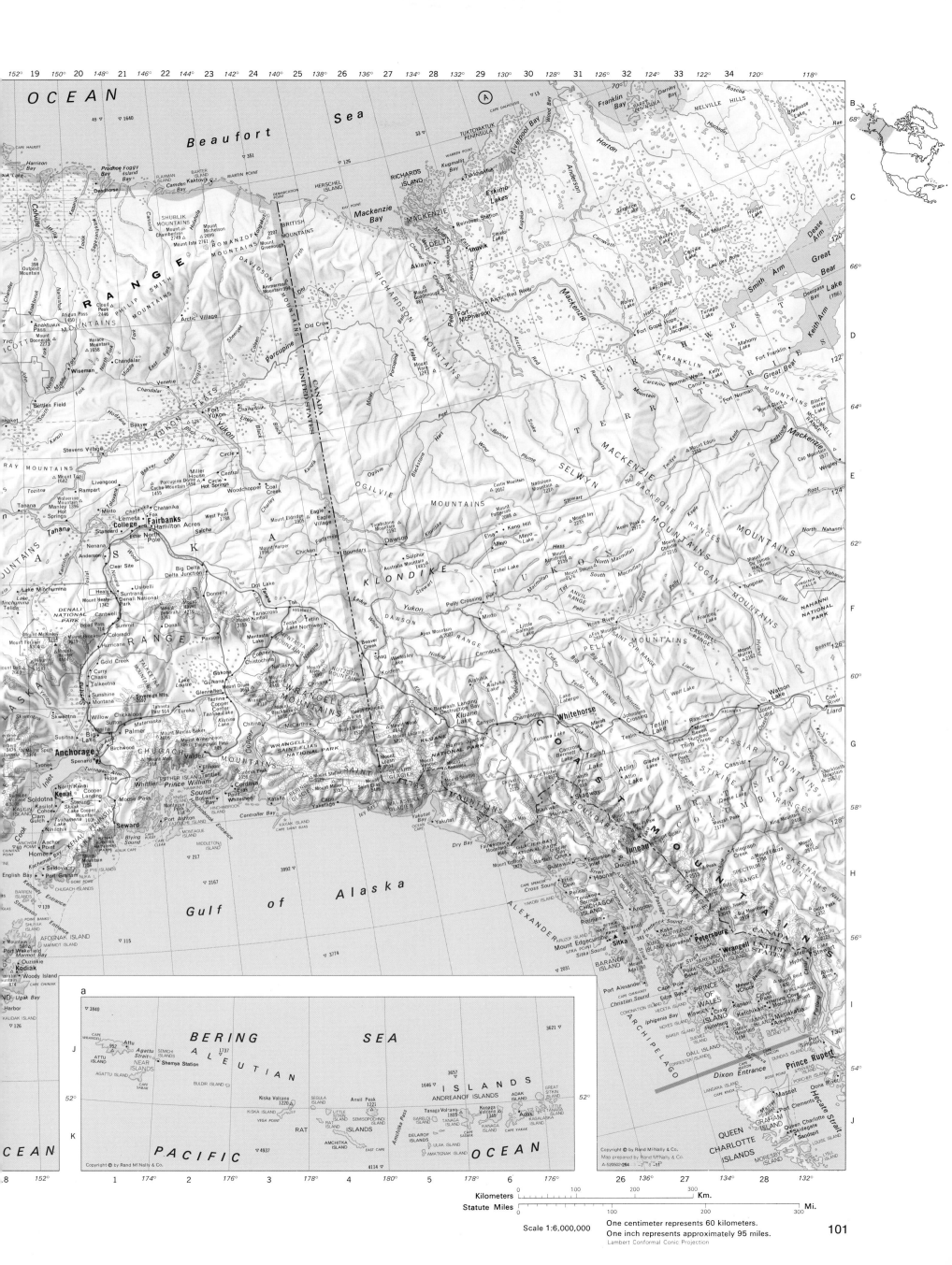

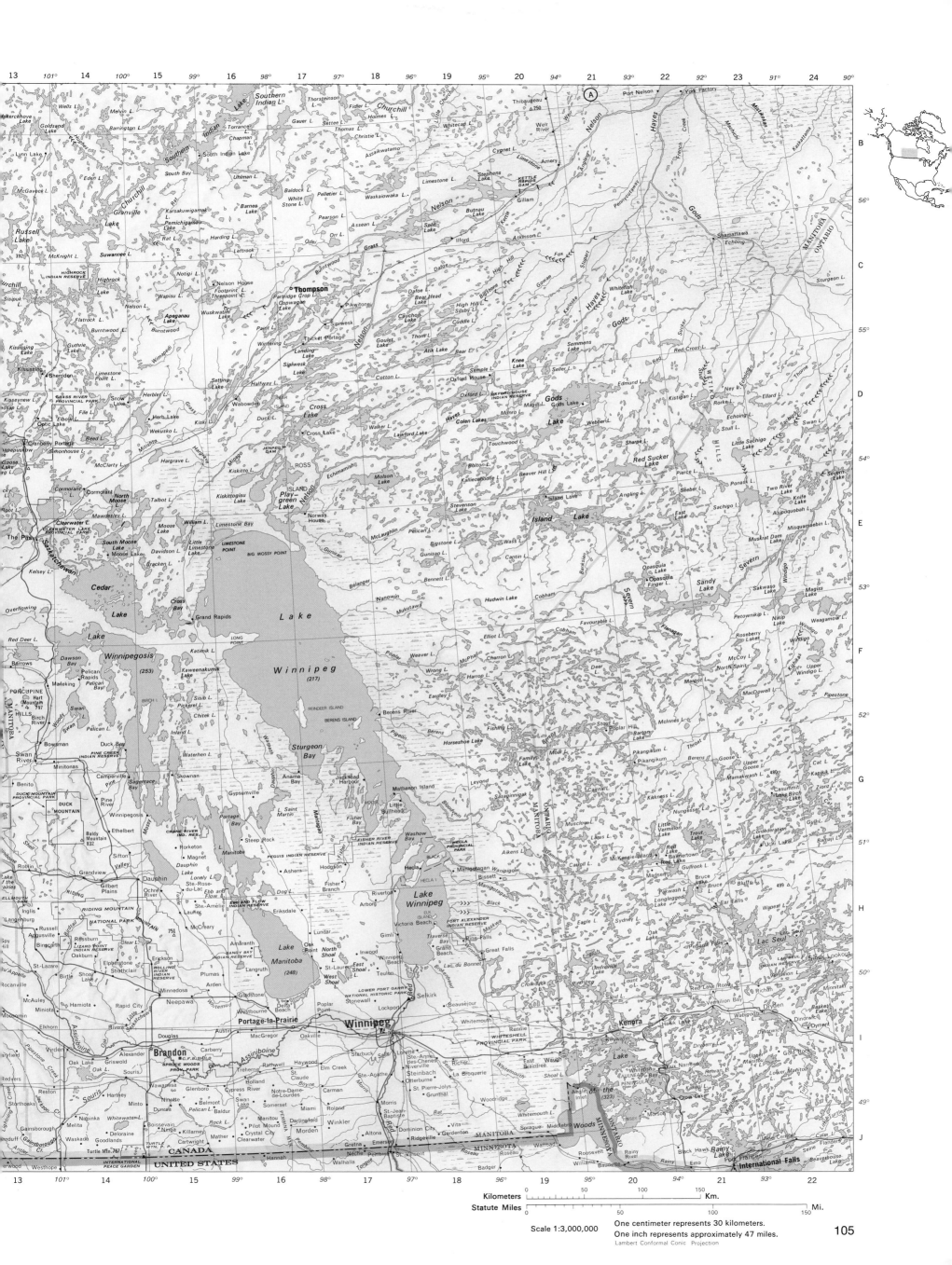

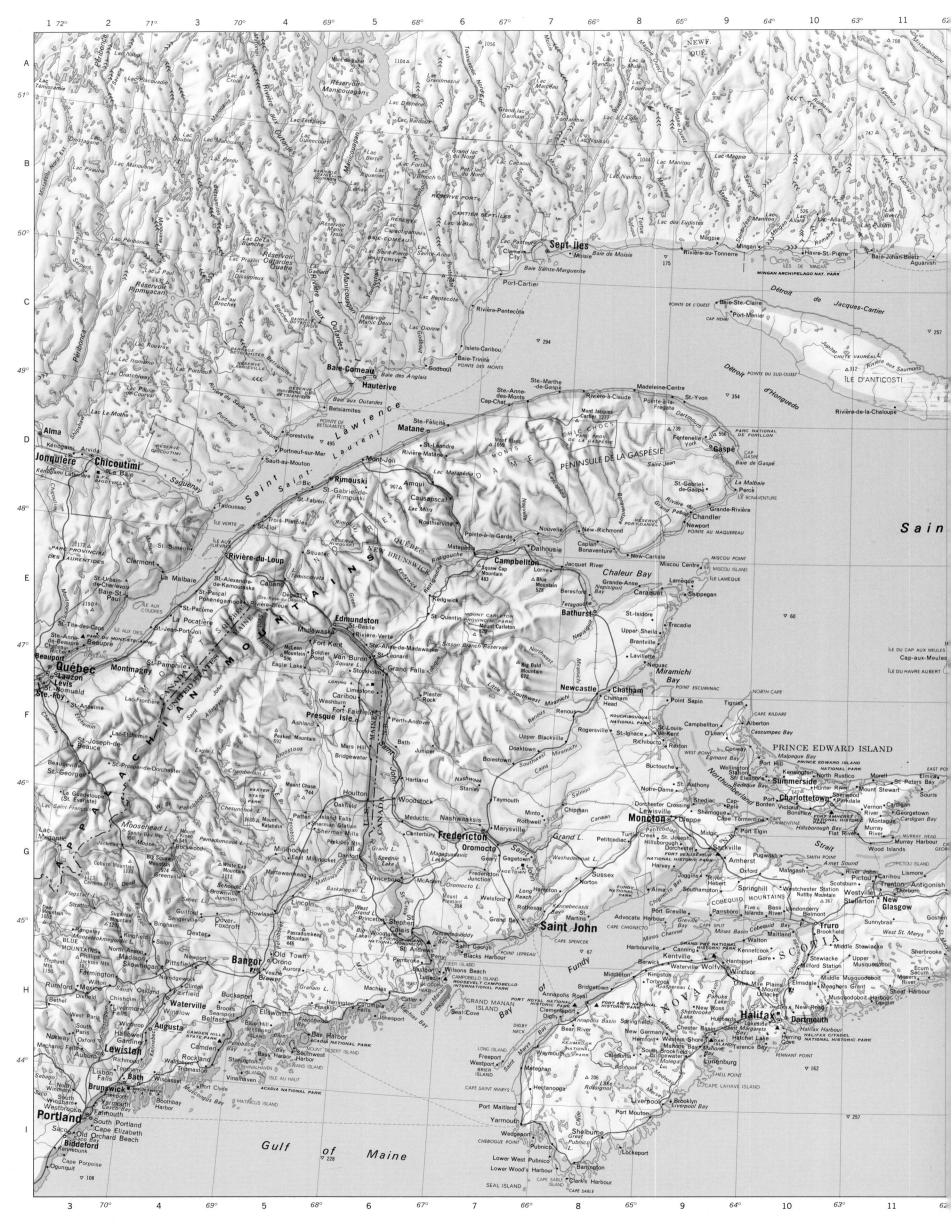

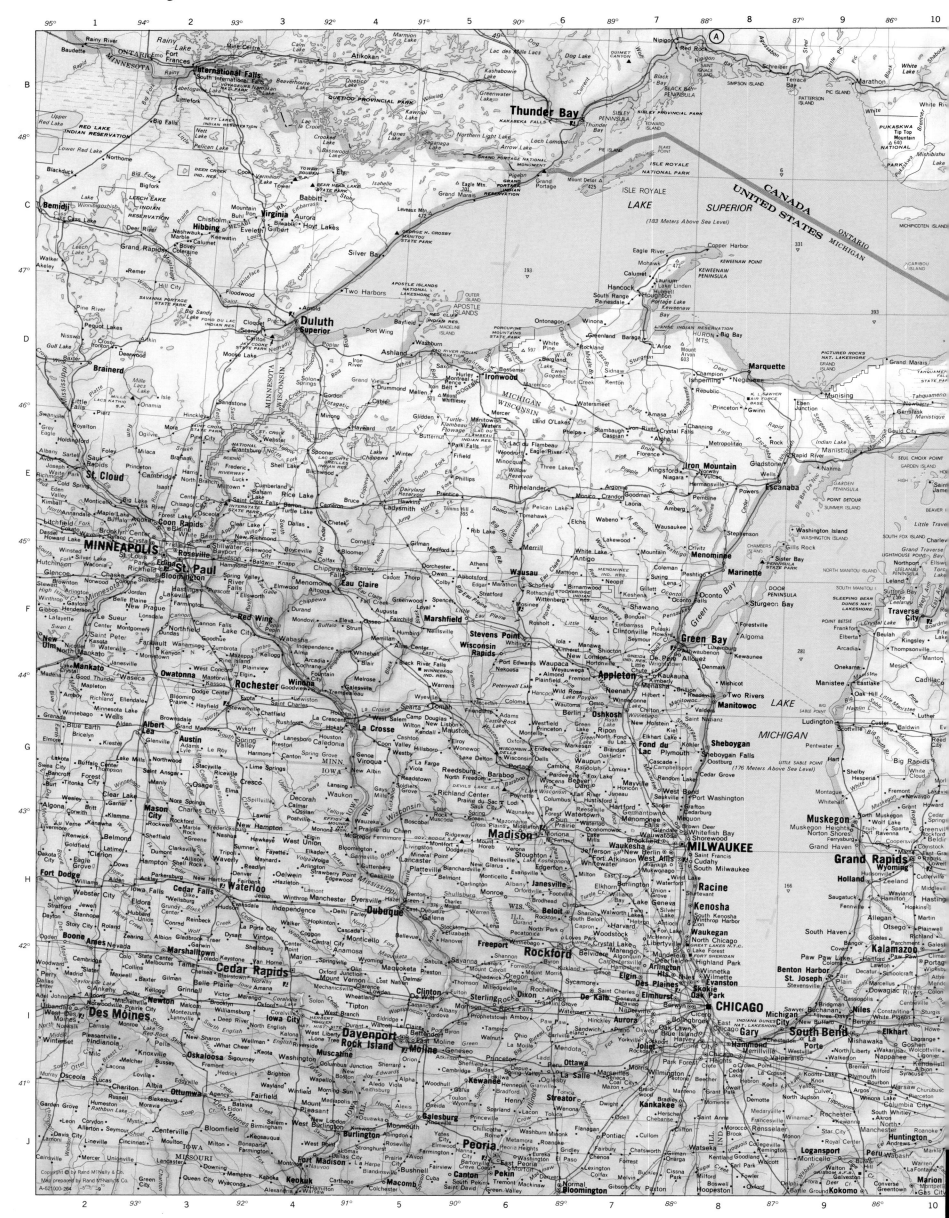

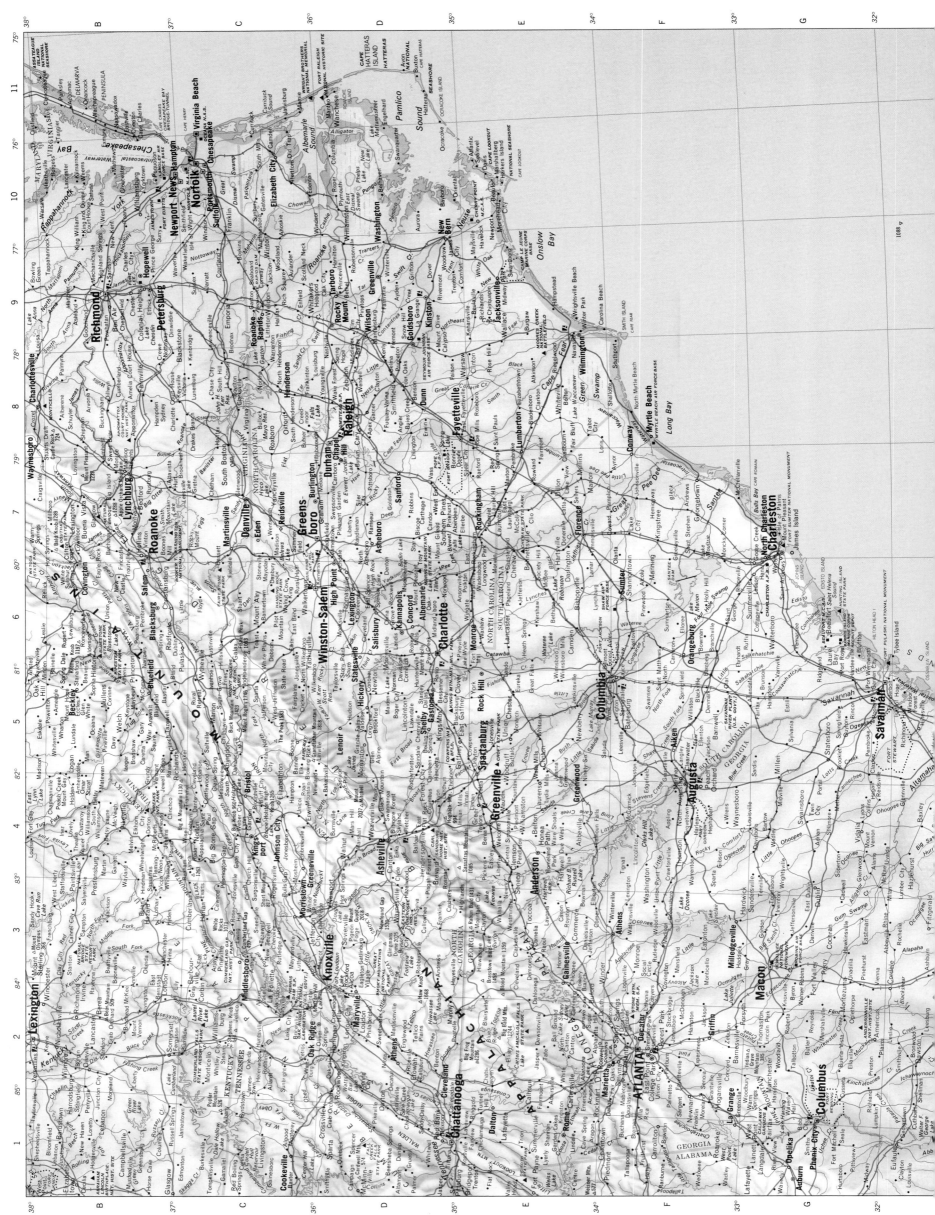

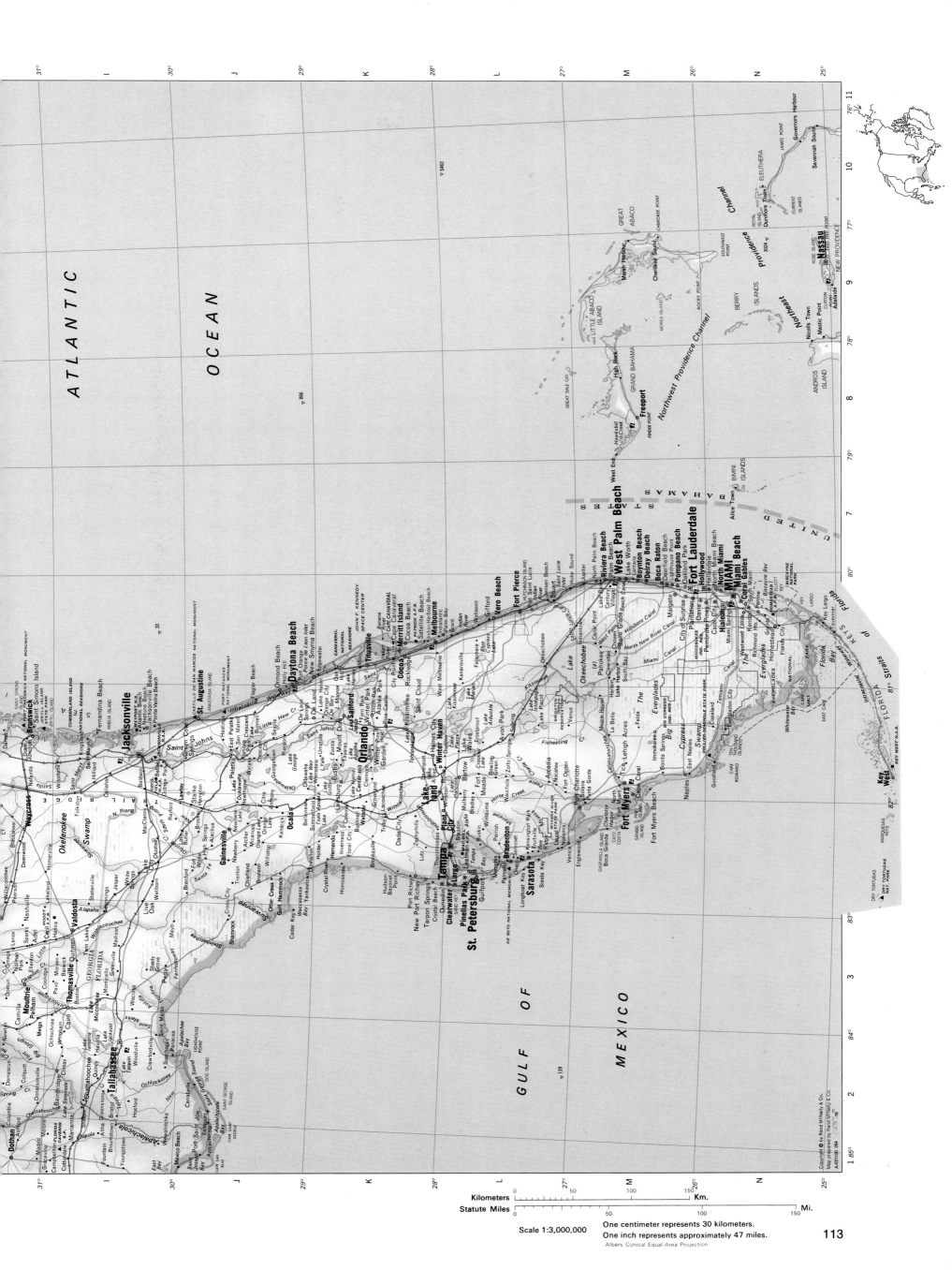

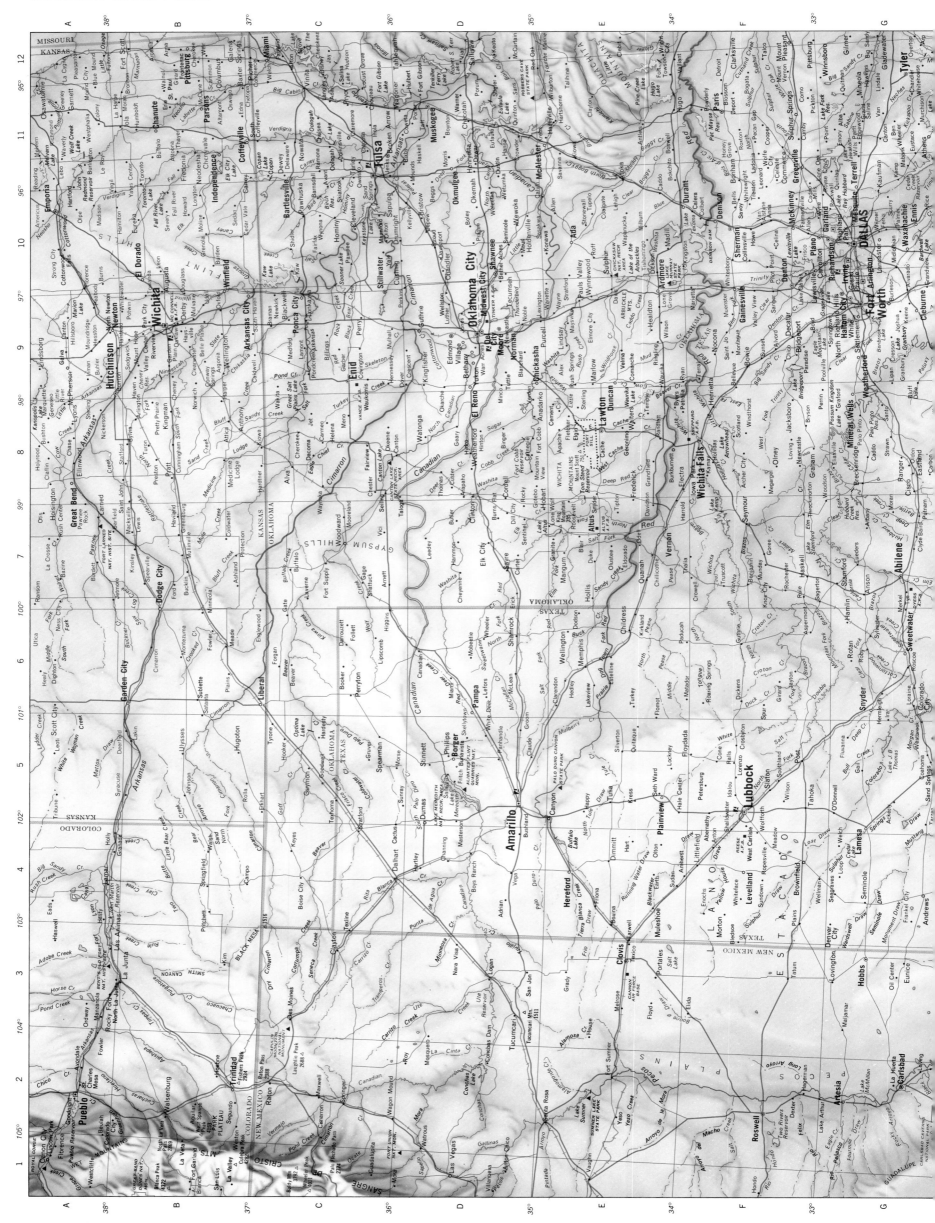

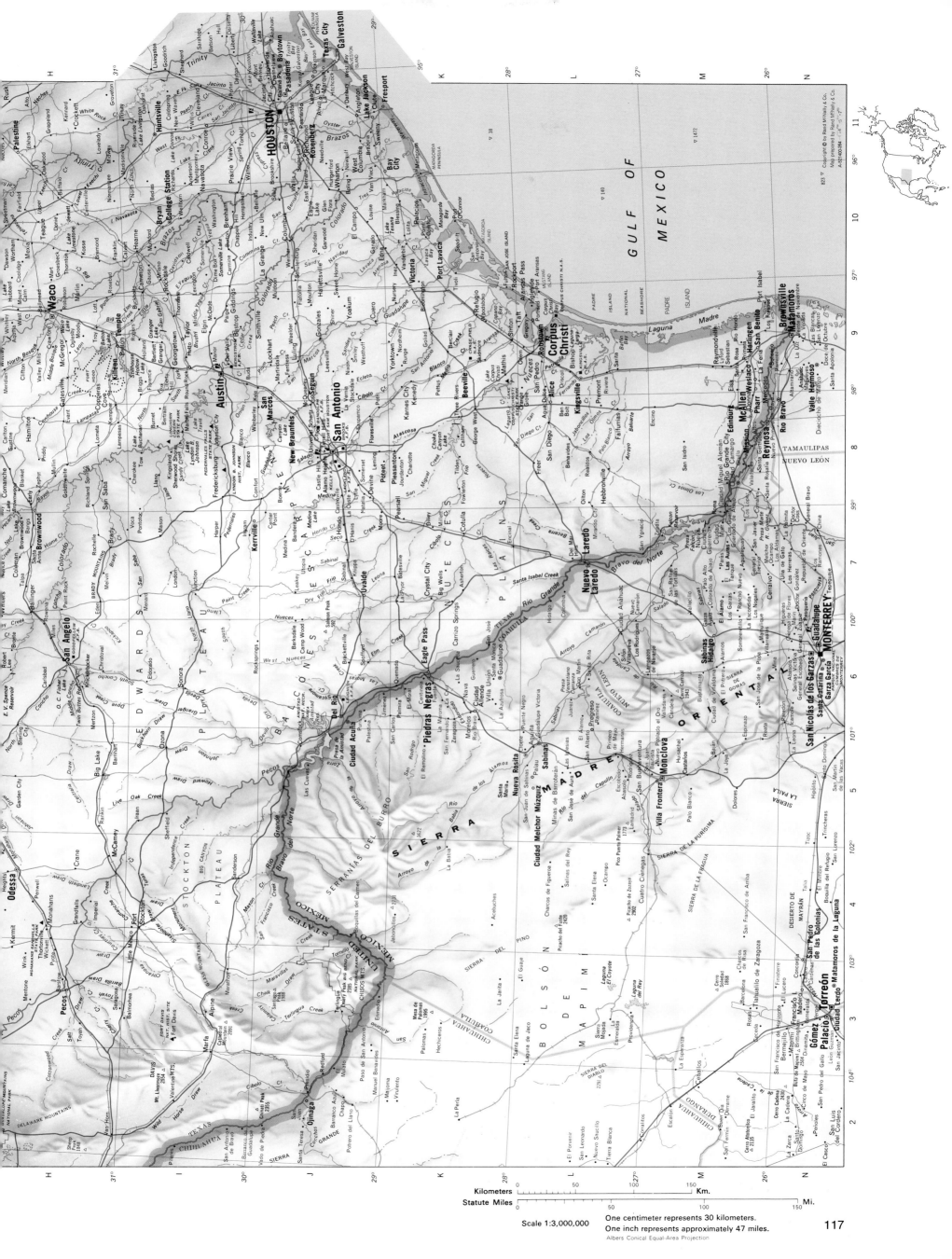

Kilometers

Statute Miles

One centimeter represents 30 kilometers.
One inch represents approximately 47 miles.

Scale 1:3,000,000

Albers Conical Equal-Area Projection

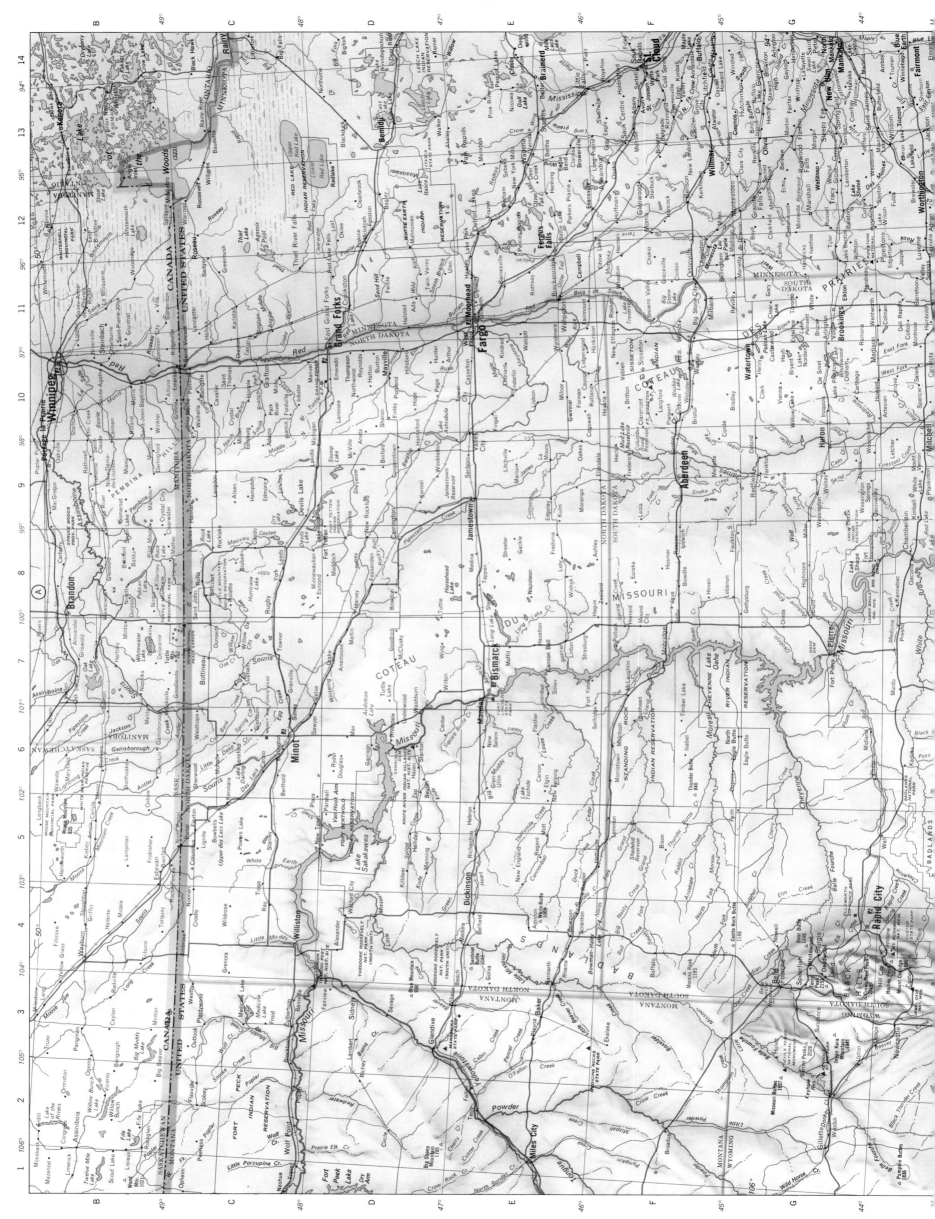

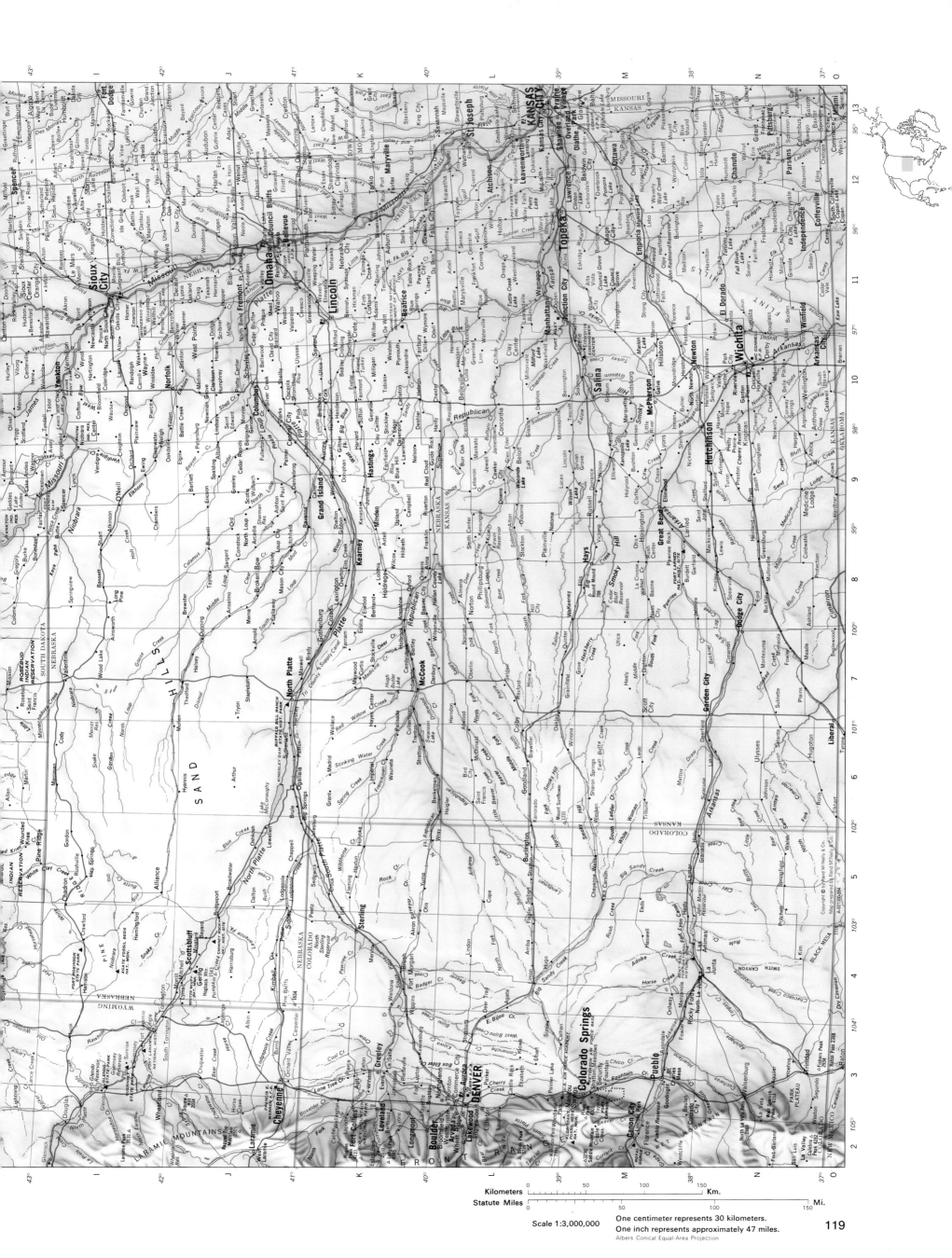

Kilometers
Statute Miles

Scale 1:3,000,000

One centimeter represents 30 kilometers.
One inch represents approximately 47 miles.

Albers Conical Equal-Area Projection

Copyright by Rand McNally & Co.
Map prepared by Rand McNally & Co.
A-821300-284

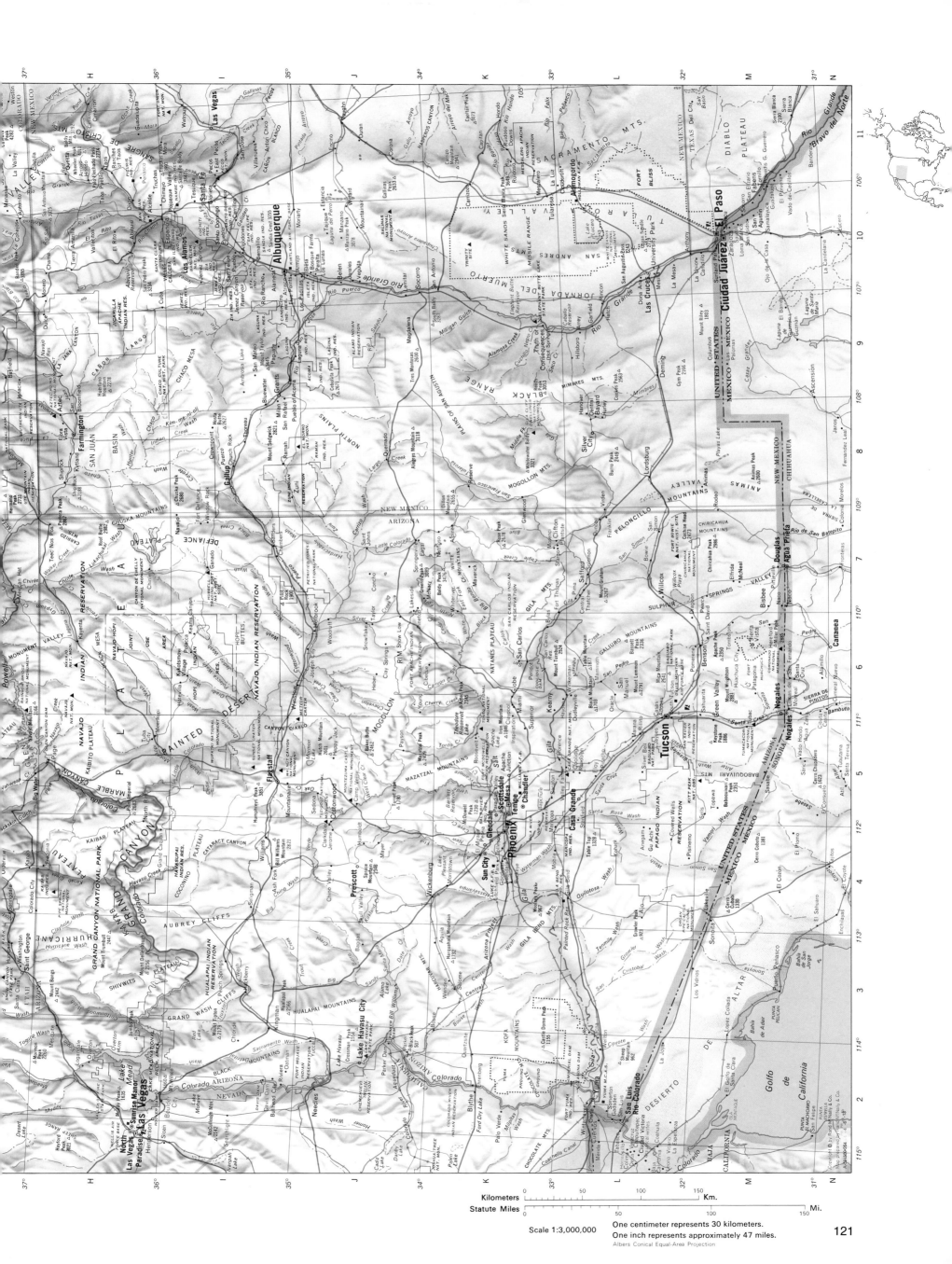

Scale 1:3,000,000

One centimeter represents 30 kilometers.
One inch represents approximately 47 miles.

Albers Conical Equal-Area Projection

Kilometers

Statute Miles

0   50   100   150 Km.

0   50   100   150 Mi.

Scale 1:3,000,000

Kilometers

Km.

Statute Miles

Mi.

One centimeter represents 30 kilometers.
One inch represents approximately 47 miles.

Albers Conical Equal-Area Projection

123

Kilometers

Statute Miles

Scale 1:3,000,000

One centimeter represents 30 kilometers.
One inch represents approximately 47 miles.

Albers Conical Equal-Area Projection

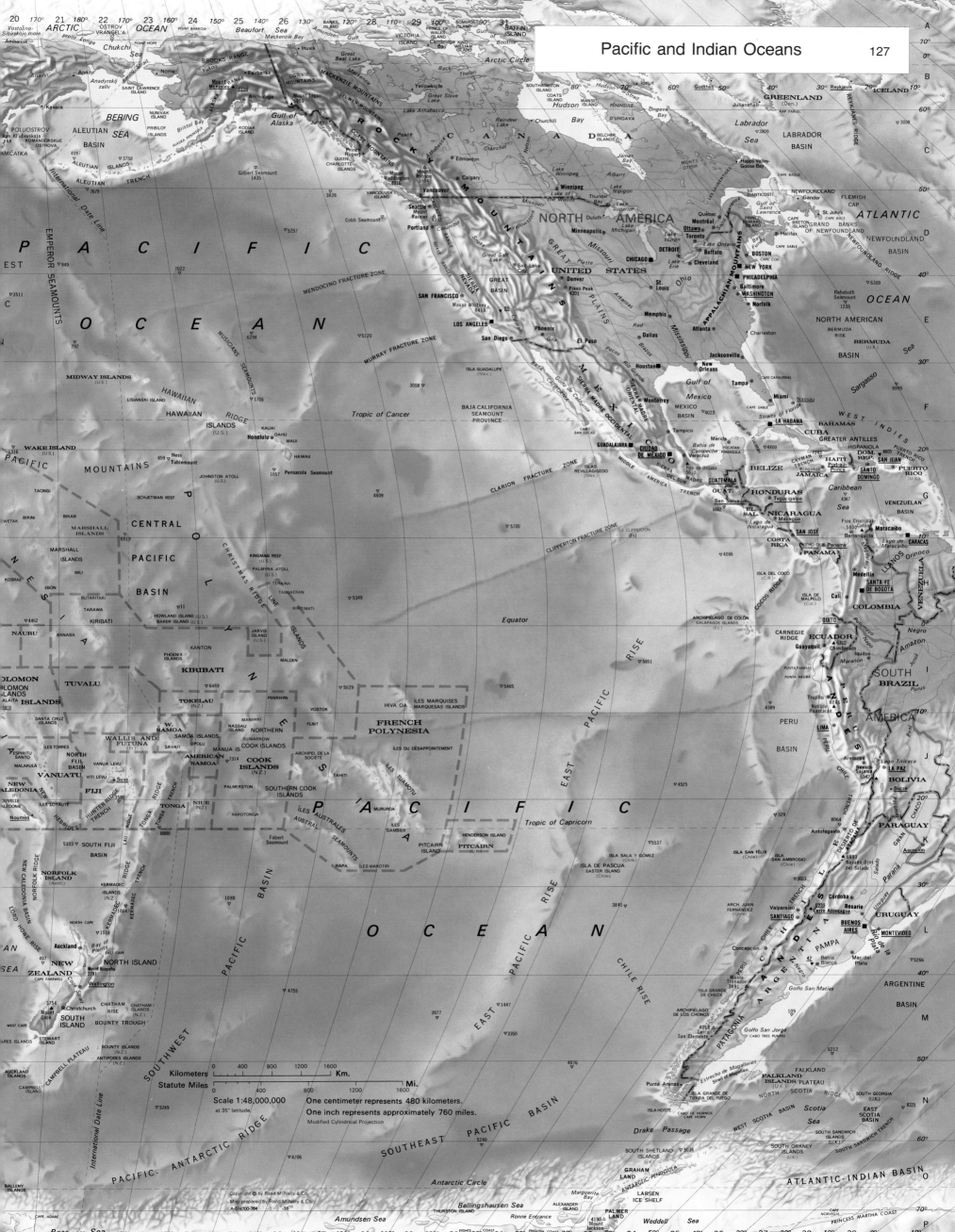

Scale 1:48,000,000
One centimeter represents 480 kilometers.
at 35° latitude
One inch represents approximately 760 miles.
Modified Cylindrical Projection